UNCOMFORTABLE CONVERSATIONS WITH A BLACK BOY

UNCOMFORTABLE CONVERSATIONS WITH A BLACK BOY

EMMANUEL ACHO

MACMILLAN

First Published in the US 2021 by Roaring Brook Press

First Published in the UK 2021 by Macmillan Children's Books
an imprint of Pan Macmillan
The Smithson, 6 Briset Street, London EC1M 5NR
EU representative: Macmillan Publishers Ireland Limited,
Mallard Lodge, Lansdowne Village, Dublin 4
Associated companies throughout the world
www.panmacmillan.com

ISBN 978-1-5290-6773-6

1 3 5 7 9 8 6 4 2

A CIP catalogue record for this book is available from the British Library.

Printed and bound by CPI Group (UK) Ltd, Croydon CR0 4YY

Visit www.panmacmillan.com to read more about all our books
and to buy them. You will also find features, author interviews and
news of any author events, and you can sign up for e-newsletters
so that you're always first to hear about our new releases.

TO OUR YOUTH,
OUR FUTURE HEROES

CONTENTS

INTRODUCTION

Young peoples!

The first thing I want you to know is, I get it. I prrrrrrromise you, I get it. Because I went through it. We're all a little unsure of who we are right now. Unsure of who we're supposed to be or who we're going to become. We are all either going through that awkward phase, about to head into that awkward phase, or just coming out of it. Trust me, I know what I'm talking about. There was a time when I was insecure. I was the black kid at the predominantly white private school—St. Mark's School of Texas—who stuck out like a sore thumb. Yet, I was also a black kid who went to a predominantly black church, but I wasn't exactly "black cultured." So at church, whose congregation was mostly black Americans, I wasn't sure I fit in there either.

Add to that, I was an awkward kid who wore braces for two years—from eighth grade to tenth grade. I didn't know how to dress or carry myself with any kind of confidence.

So Monday through Friday at school, I stuck out and felt awkward. And Sunday at church, I stuck out and felt awkward. To be true, the only place I felt comfortable was in sports. Growing up, I did football and basketball and track, and it was the only time I felt like I knew all parts of myself completely.

Back in those days, I didn't have the language or the courage to talk about blackness or whiteness. And there were no adults talking to me about it either. Consider this book my attempt to be one of the adults who broaches those difficult conversations about race. Life is already hard enough as a young person trying to figure everything else out; the last thing we need is to make life any harder, to expect you to untangle racial issues and racial tensions America had handed you all on your own.

I can tell you that I wasn't unaware of racism growing up. My home state of Texas is the birthplace of Juneteenth—the June 19th holiday that celebrates the day enslaved people in Texas finally discovered they'd been set free by the Emancipation Proclamation, a full two years after it had been signed by Abraham Lincoln. They were the last group of black people in the country to find out. It's a day that, among other things, calls attention to the state's long Confederate history. From the time I was nine or ten years old, I began to experience racism.

It wasn't that overt, call-you-the-N-word-to-your-face type racism. It was more subtle. Like, for example, the uncountable times some kid in elementary school or middle school or high school plopped down at my lunch table, and after hearing me recount some playground story, said, "You don't even talk like you're black," or "You don't sound black," or "You don't even dress like you're black." Or the ever-popular "You're like an Oreo: black on the outside, white on the inside." Unfortunately, I'm sure you've either heard this or said it yourself. Or the time after we watched the movie *Roots*—a movie that tells the story of a black man captured in Africa in 1750 and enslaved in America, and what happens to generations of his family—and people started coming up to me saying, "My name is Toby" (a line from the movie where the plantation overseer is beating an enslaved man to make him accept his new, slave name), which was straight up a joke about slavery. To be clear, young peoples, these racist insults were wrong and deeply hurtful to me. My white classmates taunted and teased me because I didn't meet their racist stereotypes of what a black person should be. That kind of behavior is never okay.

After my time at St. Mark's, I ended up at the University of Texas and found myself surrounded by more black people than I ever had been before. *Yo*, I realized, *these are my people.* Those early college years were the first time I truly understood what it meant to be a black man in America. Part of this meant realizing how my childhood had given me misguided impressions about my own people. I had been fed the same stereotypical stuff about black people as the white kids around me, and I hadn't been immune. The way my peers picked apart the way I looked, the way I sounded, the way I acted, they'd got me under the impression that the only *real* way to be black was to be like Tupac or Nelly (you might know him from *Dancing with the Stars*, but when I was a kid back in 2002, he was a popular rapper). But finally surrounded by so many students who looked like me, so many different expressions of blackness, I knew I was just fine the way I was. But I started to wonder: If I, a second-generation black man, could be taught to believe distorted things in such a short time, how much easier is it for a white person to believe them?

Today, I'm grateful for all my experiences, because

they were good lessons. Some of you might be studying a foreign language right now. Well, your teacher might have already told you: To be fluent in a language, you have to study abroad. I studied Spanish all four years of high school. "Manuelito" was my Spanish name in class. I even got kicked out of class a couple of times by Mrs. Hiner for being a class clown, but that's a story for another book. Even though I studied Spanish for four years, I was never fluent because I never set foot in Spanish-speaking country. Well, during my childhood, living in a predominantly white neighborhood, I was fluent in white culture—and then I studied abroad in black culture during college and during my years playing in the NFL. I played on teams where 80–90 percent of the players were black, each of whom brought along his own experience of being a person of color in America. Now, I'm fluent in both cultures: black and white.

The book you're reading is what I want to do with that perspective.

The COVID-19 pandemic of 2020 will go down as one of the greatest pandemics in recent history. I'm still not sure how y'all went to school from home for so long. (How many times did your grown-ups tell you to "wear your masks and wash your hands" back in 2020?)

However, the longest-lasting pandemic in this country is a virus not of the body but of the mind, and it's called *racism*. I'm not sure if we can cure racism completely, but I believe that just as scientists rushed to find a vaccine for COVID-19, we should be equally steadfast in finding a cure for the virus of racism and oppression. However, this time around *you* are the scientist tasked with finding the cure, and get this, you don't even have to go to med school.

Dr. Martin Luther King Jr. once said, "The ultimate logic of racism is genocide." I don't mean to be that guy, but we are living in an America where a white police officer felt comfortable kneeling on the neck of an unarmed black man named George Floyd for over eight whole minutes until he died. And the officer did it in broad daylight! In front of witnesses he knew were recording his actions! This is why America needs the Black Lives Matter movement. This is why, in 2020, in the middle of a pandemic, America erupted in nationwide protests against police brutality. And this is why the simple declaration, "black lives matter"—that *people who look like me are worth saving*—has become controversial.

I want to be an agent of change, want to help cure the systemic injustices that have led to the tragic deaths of too many of my black brothers and sisters; from prisons popping up around the country like fast-food chains; to inequalities in health care and education; to the often unseen racism behind who gets to live where; to the ingrained ignorance of Americans who can't see beyond skin color. I believe an important part of the cure we're looking for, maybe the most crucial part of it, is to talk to each other.

Let me take a second to break down what I mean. I don't mean just casual chatting; I mean a two-way dialogue based on trust and respect, a give-and-take conversation where all parties share their perspectives and trade information. The goal here is to build relationships—and ultimately, to help us recognize each other's humanity. Remember the new kid at school, how you thought they were a little bit different until you actually took time to talk to them and quickly realized they were more similar to you than you thought. That's the same goal here, to ask questions and get some questions answered, because we're all more similar than we are different.

In this book, the only bad question is the unasked question. If you've seen my video series, *Uncomfortable Conversations with a Black Man*, on social media, then you know I believe real change begins with thoughtful discussions over hard questions. During each video, I speak to white people who want to understand black Americans and our experience in this country better. We talk about racism, culture, and history. And we talk about solutions that will help lift our country out of the current mess it's in. You, my young friend, are a part of the solution.

If things go the way I hope they do, you will leave this book with more confidence in yourself and how to treat people who don't look like you. You will have more empathy and grant people more grace. And if you have more empathy and are more gracious, then you'll be less judgmental. And if you're less judgmental, then your judgment is less likely to play itself out in racist ways.

Racism comes in many forms. To understand what I mean, I think it's helpful to imagine racism as a very ugly building with three floors. Enter the building and you're on the first floor, where the white-hood-wearing, cross-burning, Confederate-statue-defending, tiki-torch-toting, N-word-barking racists hang out.

They believe their skin color or DNA makes them superior to others. Think of these people as the type of folks who would join a white supremacist group or attend a hate-filled rally against immigrants. Now run to the elevator, quick, before they see you.

When the elevator door opens to the second floor, things appear a little different. Look around and you won't see Confederate flags waving (more on *that* later), or hear people boasting about the size of their Nazi tattoos. Instead, you see regular folks going about their everyday business. But if you peered inside their minds, you'd see that second-floor racists believe, with their whole hearts, very negative ideas— what folks call *biases*, or as they said back in the day, *stereotypes*—about people from other racial groups or ethnicities. They may condemn organized hate groups like the KKK, but the folks on the second floor are holding on to some of the same ideas that you might hear shouted out at a Klan rally. Sometimes they may act on their racism by refusing to hire or work with people because of their skin color or foreign-sounding accents. They may even believe overly simplistic ideas like "black families are dysfunctional," or "black culture is bad," or even "illegal immigrants bring crime." Applying these stereotypes to entire groups of people—*millions!*—without having any real factual evidence to back them up. I know, these ideas stink. Moving on to the third floor!

Up here reside the people who are not visibly racist or holding on to harsh opinions about other racial groups, yet they're still a little racially insensitive, ignorant, or somewhere in between. In other words, it's usually not their intention to hurt people with their words or actions, but sometimes they do. What they don't realize is that just by living in this culture, they have become fluent in the language of racism. That's because racism has been a part of our country's culture from the very beginning—more on this later. Folks on this floor may say things like, "I don't see color, I just see human" or "Racism isn't a problem anymore, because Dr. King fixed all of that in the sixties." Crazy, right? If Dr. King fixed everything in the sixties, we wouldn't still be having these conversations today.

I know that's a lot to take in, but perhaps one of those descriptions might fit you or someone you know. If your answer is "yes" or "maybe" or "I'm not sure," just relax and take a deep breath, because I got you. You don't have to stay here. Just keep reading.

Let's take a pause—are you uncomfortable yet? Look, I won't lie to you, we're only getting further in the weeds from here. We're going to talk about slavery a lot. We're going to talk about privilege. And complicity. And so on.

BUT: Getting uncomfortable is the whole idea. Everything great is birthed through discomfort. Think about it—I endured years and years of grueling football practices, many of them under a scorching Texas sun, before I made it to the NFL. I suffered through twenty-six months of braces, power bands included, to get my million-dollar smile (minus a few cents; I wasn't very disciplined). Most of our major accomplishments are accompanied by some form of discomfort. If we truly want to cure this four-hundred-year American virus, which has been infecting this country since the first stolen Africans landed in Jamestown in 1619, then we all are going to have to buckle in.

In his poem "Let America Be America Again," Langston Hughes writes, "O, let America be America again— / The land that never has been yet—" Hughes published these words in 1936, a time when Jim Crow laws, formal and informal, still ravaged the country and he had strong reason to criticize America for not fulfilling its promise to *all* of its citizens. And almost thirty years later, in 1965, when civil rights leader and future senator John Lewis, then just a college student, led over five hundred marchers in Selma, Alabama, to protest segregation, white people were *still* unwilling to make America what it could be. Instead, the marchers were greeted on the other side of the bridge with tear gas and angry police officers who beat them with clubs.

Even fifty-six years after Langston Hughes published his poem, the version of America he was looking for still hadn't arrived. By the time of the 1992 Los Angeles uprising, when people took to the streets in protest after four police officers were cleared of all charges after brutally beating an unarmed black man named Rodney King for fifteen minutes (sound familiar?), scores of white people were still resistant to forging a version of America that made good on its founding principles. In 2016, when NFL player Colin Kaepernick, and later others, started kneeling during the playing of the national anthem to protest police brutality, white America showed that they were dramatically divided on accepting how far America still has to go. Now it's 2021, the beginning of a new decade: over eight decades after Hughes's poem. In the wake of the devastating murder of George Floyd, I believe the majority of white Americans are now ready to help America become the land it dreamed for itself.

It's going to take all of us—you, me, little kids, adults, everybody—to achieve the dream. You are going to have to learn how to move beyond being *not* racist, or "seeing everybody equally," to being *anti*-racist (a term that's been around for decades, but was recently made popular by scholar Ibram X. Kendi). If you're reading these words, I'm going to venture that you might be ready to see the America that Langston Hughes challenged us all to will into existence. Huddle up, my young friends. It starts with an uncomfortable conversation.

I don't proclaim to have all the answers, but I do pledge to share what I've learned in order to help you figure some things out about whiteness and blackness.

Thank you in advance for listening, sharing, and believing. Let's change the world—together.

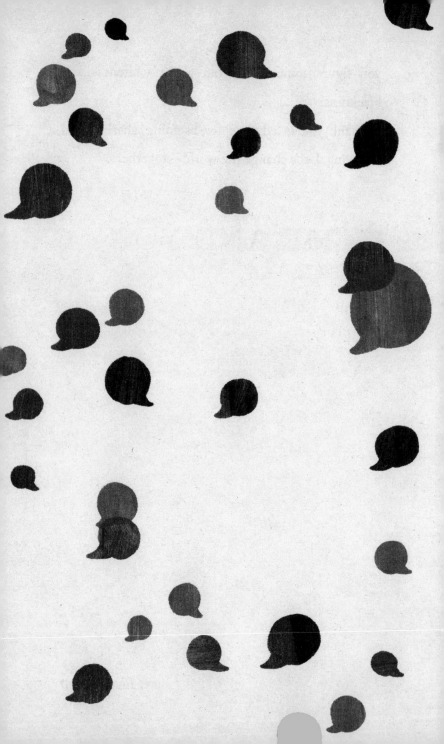

PART I

ME AND YOU

THE BIRTH OF WHITENESS

All men are created equal, unless we
decide you are not a man.

—COLSON WHITEHEAD,
The Underground Railroad

To understand what race means in America today, we must go way back to the beginning. Before enslavement was a lifelong sentence. Before slavery was based solely on skin color. Before the invention of racial labels like *black* and *white*. We must go back to the late 1600s, to the English colony of Virginia, before there even was a United States of America. We must go back to the invention of whiteness.

The first enslaved people from Africa were brought to the English colonies in 1619. They were forced to work the fields of rich European—they weren't yet considered white—landowners along with enslaved Native Americans and indentured servants (poor Europeans who agreed to work for a set number of years in exchange for travel to the colonies, lodgings, food, and their own land at the end of their indenture). At this time, many enslaved Africans worked under similar terms as indentured servants. Sometimes they could work extra jobs over the years of their enslavement to earn enough money to purchase their freedom.

The poor—the indentured Europeans, the enslaved Africans, and the enslaved Native Americans— all labored alongside each other for rich European landowners. The conditions were harsh, to say the least. Back then, the land was swampy and full of disease-causing insects, and most died before ever earning their freedom. Despite their hardships, many poor workers tried to build lives for themselves. Some got married, sometimes to people with different skin tones—color didn't matter because race and racism hadn't been invented yet. Sure, people *saw* skin color, but they didn't see racial labels like *black* and *white*. Not yet. Instead they saw human beings whose skin tones were shades of ivory, beige, tan, and brown. Not distinct groups separated by a physical trait, a phenotype.

As the colonies grew, so did the greed of the landowners. They took more and more land from the Native Americans, who had lived on and cared for it for thousands of years prior. But as the poor workers became free of indentured servitude, they wanted land, too. However, there wasn't much to be had, since the rich landowners refused to give newly freed men the land that they were promised, keeping the best land for themselves. Meanwhile, the native people fought hard to keep what lands they had left. As you might imagine, the poor workers grew angry and hopeless. For years, they'd toiled to make other men rich, and now there was little to nothing left for them. How were they supposed to provide for their families if there was no workable land for them to own and make a living from? Desperate, in 1676, the poor—African *and* European—united and organized an uprising in Jamestown, Virginia, which we know today as Bacon's Rebellion, a bloody fight that *almost* succeeded in overthrowing the rich landowners.

The group of rebels first took out their misplaced anger on nearby Native American villages, killing men, women, and children. They intended to take their land by force. When the governor of Virginia colony, William Berkeley, ordered them to stop, the rioters marched to Jamestown instead and set it on fire. Berkeley and the other rich landowners managed to stop the rebellion with the help of a British gunship, but just barely.

Scared that their plantations and profits were about to go up in smoke, rich Virginia landowners schemed between themselves. They wanted to devise a plan to keep the poor from ever uniting together again in revolt. *We must separate the poor*, they thought.

What happened next was the beginning of the invention of race as we know it today. In 1681, the word *white* appeared for the first time as a label for an entire group of people. Europeans were no longer just French, English, German, or Dutch. Now under the law, they were all part of this new group called *white*. And the inventiveness of the rich white landowners didn't stop there. Enslaved people from Africa were no longer seen as distinct persons from different cultures like Ndongo, Igbo, or Yoruba. With the stroke of a pen—or, more accurately, a quill—they became *blacks* or *Negroes*. New laws barred people from these newly created races from marrying outside of their group. Poor whites were given positions of authority over blacks. Race-based laws also prevented blacks and Native Americans from testifying against whites in courts, owning property, or holding certain jobs. With each passing law, the freedom of black people and Native Americans dwindled, while white people received more privileges based solely on being part of the "supreme," or favored, group. By the 1700s, most colonial laws stated only blacks could be enslaved for life and that any child born to an enslaved woman was also a slave.

These race-based laws grew into a system of racism called *white supremacy* that continues to take away freedom and opportunities from non-white people, while giving advantages to white people for centuries to come.

"What terms are acceptable now to refer to black people and why has that changed over time?"

1 ROLL CALL

Black or African American?

According to my Teachers,
I am now an African-American.
They call me out of my name.
BLACK is an open umbrella.
I am a Black and A Black forever.
I am one of The Blacks.

—GWENDOLYN BROOKS, "I AM A BLACK"

On May 25, 2020, a black man named George Floyd died at the hands of police officers after being handcuffed and pinned to the ground. One of the officers, Derek Chauvin, kneeled on Floyd's neck for eight full minutes, slowly suffocating George to death. Some witnesses to this horrific act recorded the incident. The next day, the video went viral. It shocked the world. And sparked nationwide protests against police brutality.

Weeks later, Washington, D.C., city workers painted three bold words down the street leading directly to the White House: BLACK LIVES MATTER. The city had already renamed this section of D.C.'s Sixteenth Street to Black Lives Matter Plaza, and now they had a two-block-long street mural so big you could see it from space. Size matters, but the heart of the mural is the language, and the key word here is this one: *black*.

We'll get (way) further into the Black Lives Matter movement, but for now, let's keep it real: "African American lives matter!" as a motto just doesn't have the same ring to it.

Giant murals aside, what do you call a person of African descent living in America: black, African American, colored, Negro? (Okay, I was just playing about the last two. Those terms been dead.) Does it matter what you call us? I want to start with this question because I get it a lot, and if we're going to have a good, long conversation, first I want you to know how I identify myself. I also want to start here because definitions are going to be important throughout this book—the words we use have power, especially around race. And none of them, these included, are simple.

LET'S REWIND

You know how when you start a new school year, and the teacher takes roll and asks people to let them know how to pronounce their name and/or if they would rather go by another name? Well, that's like a micro version of how it is for black people in this country. In the past and even now, black people have had a hard time agreeing on how to describe ourselves as a group. We must never forget that the lion's share of people of African descent living in this country had ancestors who were seized from their homeland and stripped of the core parts of their identities: kinship ties, links to a tribe, language, and so on. Most people refer to those individuals forced into bondage as *slaves*. But I'm careful to use the word *en*slaved to describe them instead. Why? Because there is a big difference between the words *slave* and *enslaved*. Calling someone a *slave* is like saying that is at the core of who they are as a person. It is like saying what is happening *to* that person is all they are. *Enslaved* says black people weren't naturally born as slaves: They were forced into slavery. In other words, *enslaved* puts the emphasis on what white people did to black people.

Enslaved African people suffered a hellish journey. When they reached the shores of what became America, they became something less than human—legally—and were deprived of the most important things that made them, *them*. We must never lose sight of the fact that this torture went on for hundreds of years. So long that the injustices and inequality those first Jamestown landowners wrought has seeped into every corner of American life since, well beyond the abolishment of slavery in 1865.

As part of establishing themselves just after the Civil War, emancipated black people began to adopt different racial labels. The first most widely used term was *colored*, because it was accepted by both white and black people and deemed inclusive of those who had mixed racial ancestry, too. *Colored* reigned supreme into the early twentieth century, and can still be found in the name of what might be the most important black organization of all time: the NAACP (the National Association for the Advancement of Colored People, founded in 1909).

W. E. B. Du Bois, a civil rights activist as well as a sociologist and founding member of the NAACP, played a key role in spurring a change from *colored* to *Negro* as the collective term for black people in America. He pitched the word *Negro* as a name, believing it clearer in meaning because it could be used as either a noun or adjective. *Negro* held on for a few decades, from the early twentieth century until the end of the civil rights movement. And then one of the chief arguments against *Negro* eventually gained the upper hand: that it was originally a term imposed by white people onto black people.

After the late 1960s, the label *black* came into its own. After the assassination of two civil rights giants—Malcolm X and Dr. Martin Luther King Jr.—and the Watts Rebellion of 1965 (most people called it a riot, but that's all about perspective), many in the black community felt powerless. They doubted that black people would ever achieve equality with white Americans. As a response to this feeling of powerlessness, the Black Power movement emerged. The movement stressed the importance of both economic and social equality. Leaders of this movement, like Angela Davis, Stokely Carmichael, and Huey P. Newton, encouraged black people to take pride in their culture, skin color, and unique history. For the very first time in this country, it was cool to be black. One of the main arguments for using *black* was that it created a parallel with *white*. The label *black* led to affirming phrases like "black is beautiful" and "I'm black and I'm proud." It birthed groups like the Black Muslims and Black Panthers, and it generally dominated throughout the 1970s and into the 1980s.

Then, in 1988, black leaders met in Chicago to discuss the "National Black Agenda," where some proposed replacing *black* with *African-American*. One of those leaders was activist and former presidential candidate Jesse Jackson (that's right, Obama was not the first to run). Jackson explained his thinking: "Just as we were called colored, but were not that, and then Negro, but not that, to be called black is just as baseless. Every ethnic group in this country has reference to some cultural base. African-Americans have hit that level of maturity." Those in favor of *African-American* over *black* argued that *black*, like *Negro*, was a label originally assigned by slave owners. They also highlighted the links between black and sin, between black and dishonesty, between black and a lack of virtue, between black and a whole bunch of negative meanings. Many of those negative ideas came from outdated Christian beliefs that taught generations of people that *white* meant "goodness" and "purity," while *black* meant the exact opposite. Black leaders in favor of the switch argued that *African-American* shook off those old beliefs and instead celebrated a cultural heritage.

Not everyone was on board with the switch—including Gwendolyn Brooks, whose poem "I AM A BLACK" started this chapter. Brooks, the first black person to win a Pulitzer Prize (1950), published a whole collection of poems called *Blacks* in 1973. Among other things, she liked how inclusive *black* was, an "open umbrella" for anyone with skin like hers. Others opposed to Jackson and his shift to *African-American* argued that its hyphenation was another way of oppressing black people: a.k.a. despite being born on American soil, you're still not *American*

American; you're this subset. And then there were some people who felt that all the name-changing business was a distraction from the real problems.

So that's where we're at, history-wise. There remain camps of those who favor *black* and those who favor *African American* (pretty sure *Negro* and *colored* won't be making any comebacks, but one never knows). You may also have heard the term *POC* or *BIPOC*—People of Color or Black, Indigenous, and People of Color. Rather than a synonym for *black*, this acronym is more a synonym for *minority*, once the go-to for anyone non-white. I prefer it to *minority*, for the record, because people of color make up the global majority!

LET'S GET UNCOMFORTABLE

I imagine some of you are thinking, *If black people can't decide which term to use, then how and why should white people be expected to know which term to use?* Point taken. But all that means is that this conversation is worth having.

Growing up, at home, I felt Nigerian, because that's what my family was—but out in the world, I felt black, because I knew that's how the rest of the world saw me. I knew this despite the fact that I wasn't even sure I knew what being black *meant* . . . like, was I black enough if I was listening to Michael Jackson and Usher instead of Drake or Lil Wayne? Whatever I doubted about the specifics, my skin color makes me a lifetime member of the club.

As for *African American*, no one represents the definition more than I do. Even as I'm now immersed in black American culture, I'm actually a dual citizen of the U.S. and Nigeria. Every year, I go back to my father's home village for a few weeks with medical workers to provide healthcare to people who need it. Still, I don't personally identify with the term *African American*. Africa is an entire continent that is home to thousands of different cultures and languages. The term *African American* suggests that there is one "African" culture or country. It ignores the uniqueness of the diverse people groups that call the continent home. So if you're gonna go there, I mean, get it right—I'm Nigerian American. I'm not from the whole continent.

To the extent I can speak for anyone else: Black is the most inclusive choice. Here's Gwendolyn Brooks again, this time from her poem "Primer for Blacks":

The word Black
has geographic power,
pulls everybody in:
Blacks here—
Blacks there—
Blacks wherever they may be.

Black covers the descendants of the people who were brought over on slave ships and forced to work on plantations, and also includes people like my parents who immigrated to the U.S.—my dad for school in

1979 and my mother in 1982. It covers all the black people in the United States and also joins them with people of African descent in Brazil, the Caribbean, Mexico, and other countries where the transatlantic slave trade spread Africans (the diaspora). It's a descriptor of what we all have in common.

There's no one label that will satisfy all (who knows, maybe there's some old person who's okay with being called *Negro*), but there is usually an opportunity to listen to how people describe themselves or to ask someone their preference whenever necessary. Yes, it might be uncomfortable, but it's the right thing to do. It's also a decision that will keep you from making mistakes, from offending someone when that's not your intent.

TALK IT, WALK IT

And when in doubt—again, just ask. Remember in school, when a substitute teacher would ask if anyone had a particular way of saying their name or even went by another name? Jennifer would say she wanted to be called Jen. Some guy named Fernando said he preferred going by Flip. Johnathan Jr. wanted to be called JJ. And the teacher, if they cared, marked those names in the roll book, and that was that. They didn't question *why* the students had those preferences; they just respected them.

The question of whether to use *black* or *African American* is ultimately a preference, one that helps a person present their identity to the world. Each person you meet might not have a preference, but maybe they do. Trust me, language matters. What's most important is this: After being labeled by others for most of their history in this country, people of African descent get to decide for themselves what they are called.

WHAT DO YOU SEE
WHEN YOU SEE ME?

"Being white, my kids struggle
to understand why skin color
matters to people who aren't. They
also want to know why there is
such a thing as 'black culture,' like
why aren't their lives, tastes, and
preferences the same as 'ours'?"

WHAT DO YOU SEE WHEN YOU SEE ME?

Implicit Bias

Prejudice is an emotional
commitment to ignorance.

—NATHAN RUTSTEIN

A few years ago, a concerned black mom went to her son's school to mention a problem that she saw with a class assignment. The students in her son's class, which included a few black kids, had created a time line of civilizations. The time line included ancient cultures, such as the Greeks, Romans, and Incas, but no African civilizations. When asked why, the school's principal, a white woman, told the mom that the omission of African civilizations from the time line wasn't about race. She insisted that the school was "just following the curriculum." According to the mom, the principal went so far as to say, "We're not talking about whether people are white or black," when they studied ancient cultures, to which the black mom shot back, "The children have eyes, and they can see. And I'd like them to see that our [African] culture was a strong, viable culture."

Why didn't the school's curriculum include African civilizations? Why didn't the teacher recognize that there were no ancient black kingdoms on the time line? And why did the principal think teachers could teach about world civilizations without thinking about race?

The short answer is that most of the students at the school were white, and the curriculum was designed with only those students in mind. Instead of changing the curriculum to better reflect all their students—

and to be more historically accurate—the principal believed that if the teachers just didn't mention race, they were being fair to everyone.

The long answer involves something called *implicit*, or unconscious, *bias*.

Let me first point out that everyone has implicit biases, including me. They're not just about race—they're your knee-jerk judgments about every superficial difference between people. And don't get me wrong: You shouldn't beat yourself up for every single biased thought or decision. If you see a clown and think, *DANGER*, look, you're not the only one. At the same time, you're responsible for your biases, if for no other reason than that there are ways to make them more conscious. And when an idea is conscious, you can change your mind.

LET'S REWIND

In December 2018, a video of a black high school wrestler at a match in New Jersey who was forced to cut his dreadlocks by a white referee went viral. The video was watched over twelve million times—yes, twelve whole million—and it led to a flurry of criticism against the referee, including charges of abuse of power and racism. According to the news coverage, Andrew Johnson, the teenage wrestler, had wrestled many times before with the same hairstyle without any problems. But during this particular match, the referee, Alan Maloney, took issue with his hair. The rules stated that "the hair, in its natural state, shall not extend below the top of an ordinary shirt collar in the back; and on the sides, the hair shall not extend below earlobe level; in the front, the hair shall not extend below the eyebrows." A picture taken right before Andrew's hair was cut shows that his hair was the appropriate length. What Maloney argued was that Johnson's hair was "unnatural" because of his locs, making it illegal, and therefore needing to be cut if Johnson wanted to compete.

Maloney gave Johnson an ultimatum and ninety

seconds to decide—either agree to cut his locs short or forfeit the match. This was a division championship match, and knowing the whole team was depending on him, Johnson allowed a trainer to cut his locs. From the video, it's obvious that he was emotionally upset to the point of tears. No other players were forced to cut their hair or wear a head covering during that match. In fact, Johnson's opponent that day had hair long enough that it flopped in front of his eyebrows several times during their match. Hair that length is illegal, according to the rules, but Maloney didn't demand that this wrestler, a white teenager, cut his hair. This is how implicit bias works: It punishes people for being different while giving people in the acceptable group a pass.

When I was in seventh grade at St. Mark's, we had a new black kid enroll in school. The kid's name was Ste'Vaughn Williams, and he spelled his first name exactly like you see it—with an apostrophe. Not only did the teachers have a hard time pronouncing his name during roll call when he first arrived but once the white kids in the school found out how he spelled his name, they started calling him Stepostrophe. True story, they didn't call him Ste'Vaughn anymore. Almost everybody called him Stepostrophe. Now, on the one hand, you could say they were enamored by the apostrophe in his name or thought giving him that nickname was an act of friendship. On the other hand, you could say it was another example of blackness and black things being mocked and disrespected—treated as "strange."

The unique spelling of Ste'Vaughn's name and the response to it by my former St. Mark's classmates connects to a 2016 article titled "Whitened Resumes: Race and Self-Preservation in the Labor Market," by professors from Harvard, Stanford, and the University of Toronto. The article shares the results of a two-year study in which people of color used whitewashed names on their résumés. ("Lamar J. Smith" became "L. James Smith," etc.) I'll give you one wild guess what the researchers discovered. Yup: Applicants with white-sounding names were more likely to be called back for an interview. And not just by a little bit. They were almost *twice* as likely to be called back.

Adding insult to injury, the research showed that companies advertising themselves as "pro-diversity" discriminated just as much, and sometimes even more! This is exhibit A of implicit bias: When a company thinks of itself as an "equal opportunity employer," or goes out of its way to say, "Minorities are strongly encouraged to apply," they may be lying and *not even realize it*. Black applicants get the false confidence that it's A-OK to reveal their race on their résumés and then, BOOM, catch a biased rejection, while pro-diversity company X wonders why they still have so few "diverse" employees.

As you probably know by now, what someone says is not necessarily a good gauge of the whole of what they think and feel or how they'll behave. And anyone can act on biases—prejudice and stereotypes—without being aware that's what they are doing. But as with "equal opportunity" employers, once bias informs our thinking, it can lead to explicit racism and bigotry.

Some of the most popular recent baby names for black boys and girls are Jevonte, Kyrone, Tamika, and Shantel. I'm willing to bet these names wouldn't have fared well on the above study. And one might say, it's just a callback for an interview—but think about all the things that can happen as a result of being *half* as likely to get that callback. That means being out of a job for longer stretches of time. If you're jobless, you're not earning money to pay your bills. And without bill money, you can't keep a roof over your family's head. Healthcare in America is often tied to a person's employer, so if you don't have a job, you might not be able to pay for medication or a simple doctor's visit.

Do you see? Are you starting to see how damaging a knee-jerk reaction can be?

Implicit bias on the job is just one source of fallout. It's also common elsewhere. Ever heard of "driving while black"? Or how hard it can be for us to catch a cab? These are old clichés for a reason—black people get pulled over way more often than white people, and we have to deal every day with the kind of snap judgment a taxi driver makes. These little slights happen constantly, and they're exhausting.

In hospitals, bias can literally determine whether a person lives or dies. Like, have a look at these findings from a report by the Center for American Progress titled *Eliminating Racial Disparities in Maternal and Infant Mortality*. It states that black women are three to four times more likely to die during pregnancy from preventable complications when compared to white women.

How can that happen? Well, black women have long been thought capable of bearing more physical pain, have received less careful, attentive, thorough healthcare, and have failed to be treated with dignity by health professionals. Those factors create a chain of biological processes known as *weathering* that undermines black women's physical and mental health. It is literally killing their babies. And a great part of why it's happening is implicit biases.

Don't get it twisted—saying these differences are due to bias isn't a way to avoid saying they're due to racism. Again, unconscious prejudices can turn into racist actions—that's the whole problem. But I think it's important to start here with the fact that you don't even have to *know* you're being racist for the damage to be done.

LET'S GET UNCOMFORTABLE

What are your implicit biases against black people and people of other races? How have those biases played out in your decision-making, in how you treat people?

Fine, I'll go first. Remember I told y'all my high school was predominantly white, and it was a small school (about eighty students per class), so new students were quickly recognized. Well, anytime there was a new black student, I would instantly try to size them up. They look a little too small to play football, I would say, but maybe they can help me out on the basketball team or the track team for sure. Based on what I had been told, about myself in particular, I began to believe that all the black students who showed up on campus must be able to run fast and jump high.

I vividly remember being surprised and a little disappointed when a student enrolled at my high school one grade below me. He looked the part. He was big, tall, and most important, he was black. I was sure we just found the new starting running back for our varsity football team, but I was appalled to find out he wasn't even fast. Talk about stereotyping gone wrong.

Years later, when I was watching the Texas High School Championships, we got to the one-hundred-meter finals. The eight lanes were filled up with the black kids I expected to see—all except lane four. "Matthew Boling?" Who was this lanky white dude? I knew he was the favorite, because lane four is always reserved for the fastest seed, but my mind instantly went back to the joke-not-joke the black sprinters on my team had: "Don't let the white kid beat you."

Now you might be thinking, why did I believe this? What fed into my bias? For decades, black runners from Jesse Owens to Michael Johnson (the track-and-field star, not the basketball player) have dominated track-and-field Olympic events. Even in college and high school sports, black runners tend to lead the pack in competitions. Based on what I thought to be true and my personal experience, I expected to see a black kid win that championship match.

Sure enough, this kid Boling ended up setting the meet record, tying the Texas state record for the one hundred meters. And to that, I say, "Touché, my white friend."

I'm sure talking about these things is uncomfortable for many of you. Especially for those of you who believe yourselves to be good people, who don't consider yourselves racist, who want to treat people fairly.

But that's all the more reason to discuss your biases, to learn about them, critique them, to try to trace where they come from. I like to use the acronym DENIAL: Don't Even kNow I Am Lying. The first way to end racism is for my white counterparts to get out of denial, to understand that, hold up, maybe you've been lying to yourself about the existence of racism this whole time. You need a counter voice in your head when you notice your internal monologue ushering you toward making a biased decision or judgment about black people. Everyone, and I mean everyone, has biases. It's the job of empathetic and considerate people not to let them dictate actions that harm others.

TALK IT, WALK IT

In order for us to conquer our implicit biases, we have to speak openly and honestly about them. Uncomfortable conversations are all about addressing this kind of thinking, airing it out. We can't let these ideas fester in silence.

So what's a game plan for reducing implicit biases?

If your school is diverse, think about joining clubs and sports teams where you can meet different people. Sit with someone new and/or different from you at lunchtime. Community centers, senior living homes, and food pantries are also great places to do volunteer work and meet lots of people different from you.

Another way is to stop celebrating "color blindness," which is the misguided idea that ignoring or overlooking racial and ethnic differences leads to racial harmony.

HGTV stars Chip and Joanna Gaines came on my show earlier last year. They wanted to be a part of my show, along with their five children, because they realized how important it is to talk about race, even if it makes us uncomfortable. Chip and Joanna told me that one day they asked their kids to pretend they saw two strangers, a black man and a white man. Would the black man make them more nervous? The kids all said no, really quickly, and the Gaineses took that as evidence that their kids were color blind—that they didn't "see race." Wasn't that a good thing, they asked? Answer: It's actually not. Not only does that overlook the difference between the experience of being black versus white in this country, "color blindness" also provides a fertile ground for implicit biases to grow unrecognized and unchecked. If you don't see someone's skin color, then you'll never recognize when you're treating them poorly because of their race.

Instead of being color blind, be introspective. Try to identify your prejudices and hold them up to scrutiny. Pay special attention to your biases when you're stressed, as that's when they are more likely to pop up without you noticing. As much as you can, try to imagine you're me—consider things from the perspective of someone you know is susceptible to discrimination or stereotyping.

Avoid lumping people into groups in general. Meet your peers as individuals. Affirm people's particularities and differences. That's what makes us human. In

your job, your school, or any other institution you belong to, be supportive of measures to diversify—along
with measures of accountability. It's like riding the
New York subway: If you see something, say something.

"My son told me that everyone can get ahead just by working hard and hustling, like he did mowing yards. But we got him started with our equipment in a neighborhood where people owned their homes, etc. It was a good conversation, but kids need to hear about fellow kids not having those same opportunities."

THE HEAD START

White Privilege

> Race doesn't really exist for you
> because it has never been a barrier.
> Black folks don't have that choice.
>
> —CHIMAMANDA NGOZI ADICHIE,
> *Americanah*

I was too big and, honestly, too slow to run track in high school, so I only watched the running events from the throwing ring with a shot put in my hand. But say you and I are in a race, and the start line official held me back for the first two hundred meters, giving you a two-hundred-meter head start. If that were to happen, the only way to level out that race is to either stop you from running or put me on a bike to catch up to you. This is white privilege in a nutshell: What we've done in America is said, "Okay, Emmanuel, you're free to run." Meanwhile, we've acted as if it's been a fair race, when in all honesty, black people were held back for hundreds of years. And still are.

Consider that after the Civil War ended in 1865, enslaved people were officially freed and made American citizens by the passing of the Thirteenth and Fourteenth Amendments. That was the starting gun. Only, just as black people were getting started, white America moved back the starting line. They had promised newly freed black people "forty acres and a mule"—parcels of land on which they could build wealth for their families and communities. But when it came time to turn that land over, white people instead gave it to those who started the war. Now, with the starting line one hundred meters back, black people also had to watch out for hurdles—like laws that make it hard to vote. Like Jim Crow laws to keep them poor and indebted, sharecropping for generations on land they didn't even own.

Then in the early 1900s, white America basically admitted they had created Jim Crow laws to keep white and black people segregated, to keep black people behind in the race. They said, "Yeah, we created laws that keep you poor and take away your rights as Americans. But run faster and catch up if you can."

So black people ran faster. Ran harder.

Later in the 1960s, white America said, "Okay, black people, you all can really go now. We've signed the Civil Rights and Voting Rights Acts. Run harder and faster." But how could two laws—as important as they are—undo four hundred years of slavery and segregation? They couldn't. And the belief by some that they could was so offensive that even President Lyndon B. Johnson felt compelled to speak about it. "You can't shackle and chain someone for hundreds of years, liberate them to compete freely with the rest, and still justly believe that you've been fair," said Johnson.

You might be wondering, "Okay, so that's the history, but what about now? What about poor white people, how can they still be 'privileged'? What about rich and powerful black people? Are they still *un*-privileged?"

The short answer is: Remember what I said about the race. It started over four hundred years ago, and there are no redos. White privilege is about the word *white*, not *rich*. It's having an advantage that's been intrinsically built into your life. It's not saying your life hasn't been hard; it's saying your skin color hasn't contributed to the difficulty in your life.

LET'S REWIND

While the term existed before her, scholar Peggy McIntosh is credited with igniting a broad conversation around white privilege in her groundbreaking 1988 essay, "White Privilege: Unpacking the Invisible Knapsack." McIntosh defines white privilege as "an invisible package of unearned assets which I can count on cashing in each day, but about which I was 'meant' to remain oblivious. White privilege is like an invisible weightless knapsack of special provisions, maps, passports, codebooks, visas, clothes, tools and blank checks."

So just what is all this backpack junk? For many white people, white privilege is the power of feeling normal. It's going to get a haircut in a barbershop or salon and not worrying if the barber or stylist knows how to cut your type of hair. It's the ability to turn on the TV and see people that look like you represented in nuanced and affirming ways. It's like having Band-Aids, or foundation colors, that match your skin. It's going to school and seeing that all or most of the grown-ups look like you. It's being in history class and seeing that all the important people and events that the teachers bother to talk about center around people like you. And it's reading books by and about people who, by and large, look like you.

In high school, we used to have pep rallies every Friday before home football games. I lived for them—I'd walk into the gymnasium, sporting my football jersey, to a roar of cheers from the whole school. The way I see this, white privilege is kind of like being on the hometown team everywhere you go. You know the fans are going to be cheering for you and that most everyone in the stands wants you to win. Everyone is ready to give you advice. Everyone likes your uniform, and you got the new helmet, pads, cleats—all the equipment you need to succeed. You're all set up to win.

Meanwhile, the road team has the secondhand pick of everything.

Another part of white privilege is the omnipresent benefit of the doubt. It's the safety of moving through the world without being singled out, without worrying that the police might harass you, or worse, just because of your skin. It's the gift of not having your complexion be the reason someone doesn't think you can afford something, doesn't show you the nice apartment, doesn't give you the loan. It's never worrying that one riot, one gang, one criminal, one *anything* halfway across the world might result in more prejudice against you, too.

If you're accused of a crime, it's the presumption of innocence until proven guilty, the presumption of innocence sometimes even when proven guilty. It's having a picture of your smiling high school graduation photo on-screen if the news ever reports you connected to a serious crime. To get back to the hypothetical game, it's like having the refs on your side. If there's a call from a referee that could go one way or another, you're pretty sure it's going to go your way. They might even bend the rules for you.

Okay, I'll stall the sports analogy. But you get what I'm saying. We'll get a lot further into how this plays out in law enforcement later, but let me give you one of the most infamous cases of "benefit of the doubt" in history. In 1955, Carolyn Bryant Donham claimed that a fourteen-year-old black boy, Emmett Till, grabbed her, menaced her, and made a sexually crude remark. Her white community believed her, and Till was captured, beaten beyond recognition, shot in the head, tied by barbed wire to a cotton gin, and thrown into Mississippi's Tallahatchie River.

None of it was true. Donham lied, pure and simple. If she hadn't, Till might be a happy grandfather right now; instead, he's a symbol of white privilege weaponized. In what's beyond a historical footnote, an all-white jury acquitted those two white men in 1956. They later admitted that they did it because they knew they couldn't be tried again because of the double jeopardy law. Donham recanted her story in 2017.

Now imagine knowing all this and walking through the world as a black boy. Imagine clocking every time a white woman crosses the sidewalk or ends up on the elevator with you; imagine having to avert your gaze so you don't make a white person uncomfortable, or changing your stride in front of police. Imagine always having to be on guard to gauge whether you are being perceived as a threat, or are in some way playing into some white person's negative image or idea of you. Look, I've played a lot of sports, and let me tell you there is no training that equals the exhaustion of having to live that kind of life all the time, not four quarters of a game but the sixteen hours or so of every day of your waking life.

Oh, and to address the rich-versus-poor question. Yes, there are poor white people, and yes, there are rich black people. But let's zoom out—white privilege is economic, too. The average net worth of a typical white family in 2016 was $171,000, a figure nearly ten times greater than that of a black family, at $17,150. TEN. TIMES. GREATER. Put another way, black people own about one tenth of the wealth of white people in this country, adjusted for population. And check this: The wealth gap persists regardless of a household's education, marital status, age, or income.

Now you tell me if the race is fair.

LET'S GET UNCOMFORTABLE

Let's talk a little bit about what academics call *intersectionality*. This refers to the ways in which the different parts of a person's identity intersect on axes of privilege and oppression and inform the ways they move through the world. For example, here are some of my privileges and how they intersect: I'm a man, for one. That means I have gender privilege. We men have been oppressing women since the earliest civilizations. Then I'm also able-bodied—this gives me able-bodied privilege. I'm from a solidly middle-class family—that's economic privilege. And I played professional football. All of those things grant me privilege in the world. So I'm not saying that a black person can't have privilege or that a white person hasn't earned anything in their life. What I'm saying is that a white person's skin color isn't the thing contributing to holding them back, but for all black people, their skin color contributes to what's hard about their lives no matter what other privileges they might enjoy.

White privilege is a hard conversation because we all want to believe in the American dream. We want to believe that America is both a democracy and a meritocracy, where all of our lives are the result of our own hard work and ambitions. I believed exactly that, all the way until I was getting my master's degree and took a class called Social Determinants of Health. Only then did I realize that not only do some people not start from zero—a lot of black people start in the negatives. And that's just not fair.

I'm hoping that if you're white and have been paying attention up to this point, you realize that, now that you know about white privilege, that makes you responsible for doing something about it? Yep, that's exactly where I'm going with this. But don't panic. This is a good thing.

TALK IT, WALK IT

When I was playing in the NFL, my "celebrity" gave me access to a secret "celebrity card" at Chipotle, one of my favorite restaurants. This card allowed me to eat at Chipotle every day for free, but more important, it gave me access to throw a party for one hundred people every year, sponsored by Chipotle. I always threw my Chipotle parties at a homeless shelter, and I invited my famous friends and teammates to join me. You see, because of my "celebrity privilege," I was granted special access in Chipotle. I didn't feel guilty about it—I had no reason to. I hadn't done anything wrong. What I did do, however, was use my privilege to benefit those around me who didn't share the same privileges.

This country won't change in a significant way until the majority of white Americans acknowledge and address their white privilege. Let's practice. If you are white in America, that means you have white privilege. It's okay to admit this. Our country was set up that way from the beginning. So if you're white and, one day, someone says, "Hey, I think your white privilege is showing," don't get angry or shut down.

Instead, focus on what that person might be feeling and experiencing based upon your actions. Learn when is the time to listen intently, when is the time to use your privilege—your home field advantage—as a megaphone for other people, and when is the time to step in and speak up. If white people are the problem, white people must also be part of the solution. I believe that.

One more thing to leave you with. I had a conversation with Carl Lentz, former pastor of Hillsong Church NYC (dude is one of the hippest pastors around) about white privilege, and he shared a conversation he had with another white man. "It's just not real," Carl quoted the man as saying.

"Okay," Carl said. "Let's just say it's not real. Let's just say I'm wrong about white privilege—but I believe in it. It means I will have lived my whole life looking out for other people. Making sure everybody else gets the first shot and I get the second. Make sure people who are not in the mix get in it." If he found out he was wrong after all that, he'd still have a life of good deeds to show for it.

On the other hand, Carl told the man, "If *you* find out that you were wrong at the end of your life, that white privilege was real and you didn't acknowledge it, it means that you were stepping on the necks of others your whole life. Even if I'm wrong, my wrong is better than your wrong. What do you have to lose?"

To all of my readers who are wavering on whether white privilege is real, I pose the same question Lentz posed to the skeptical white man. What do you have to lose by believing it?

*"Who determines what is
culturally right and wrong?"*

CITE YOUR SOURCES
OR DROP THE CLASS

Cultural Appropriation

What would America be like if we loved black
people as much as we love black culture?

—AMANDLA STENBERG

In 2014, singer Katy Perry released a music video for
her single "This Is How We Do." In the video, Perry
can be seen donning cornrows, complete with "gelled-
down baby hairs" around the crown of her do. Some
of her followers weren't impressed.

"Now that Katy Perry has cornrows, every white girl
on the planet is gonna get them."

"Katy Perry with cornrows and fake baby hairs . . . I have seen hell with my own eyes."

"I'm sorry, what? You can't take baby hairs!"

"Katy Perry wears cornrows and does a video with rappers . . . now she thinks she gets a black card? Never."

Some have called Katy Perry "pop music's queen of cultural appropriation." A repeat offender profiting from other people's culture, Perry has managed to tick off not only black people but also Asians (she dressed up like a Japanese geisha during an American Music Awards performance—yes, complete with kimono and white makeup) and Indigenous Americans (by dressing up like a "supposedly" Native woman during a 2010 trip to Coachella). In response to all the backlash, Perry got defensive, saying, "I guess I'll just stick to baseball and hot dogs, that's it."

That didn't go over very well either.

A few years ago, Perry sat down with a Black Lives Matter activist, DeRay Mckesson, to finally own up to what black women and other POC have been trying to tell her for years: Cultural appropriation is not the same as cultural appreciation. (More on that later.)

During the interview, a seemingly humbled and more introspective Katy Perry admitted her "several mistakes," saying, "I listened and I heard and I didn't know. I won't ever understand some of those things because of who I am. I will never understand, but I can educate myself, and that's what I'm trying to do along the way."

Maybe there's some hope for the "queen of cultural appropriation" after all? Time will tell. We'll be watching you, Ms. Perry.

Let me put it to you like this. I'm sure I am not the only one who's forced unnecessary quotes into a paper to meet a word count. Some of you are probably procrastinating on writing a paper right now. I feel for you. Well, when quoting someone else, your teacher probably reminded you, "Make sure you cite your sources in APA or MLA format." I'm not going to lie to y'all; I still don't know what the difference is, but I do know not citing your sources was called plagiarism and could lead to expulsion. Plagiarism, using someone else's words or ideas without attributing them, is not only considered wrong, but it has always been an offense that could get you in serious trouble. While it might be true that imitation is the highest form of flattery, plagiarism isn't flattery: it's stealing. It's doing none of the work yourself and taking as much of the credit as the world will give you. It's not knowing or caring what kind of struggle went into someone else's creation but using it to get yourself a passing grade—or a few thousand likes on Instagram.

Borrowing from or being influenced by black culture is not an issue in and of itself. The problem becomes when you borrow from a culture without citing the sources and/or knowing the history. As long as you do both of those things, you should be fine in most cases. (Key word—*most*. Not all.)

So just when does something move from homage,

creative influence, or flattery into the bad kind of copycatting—the realm of cultural appropriation? When should white people be called out for engaging with cultures that aren't theirs—and when is a braid just a braid?

LET'S REWIND

In the 1830s, a white actor named Thomas "Daddy" Rice got a bright idea. After witnessing a formerly enslaved person singing a song called "Jump Jim Crow," he created the character that would make him famous: a fictional caricature of a clumsy, dim-witted enslaved person named Jim Crow. Rice would don blackface, smearing on black, tar-like makeup and drawing exaggerated red lips, and then perform a comedic "minstrel show" mocking black people. His show was a huge hit among white audiences all over America and beyond. It wasn't long before other white minstrels were making a mockery of black people and culture and then being celebrated for it.

You probably know where Jim Crow went from there. That's right: The laws that kept the South segregated until the 1960s were named after a cruel hundred-year-old joke at the expense of black people. You know where blackface went from there, too, because we're still talking about it. The list of white public figures with blackface scandals is ever growing, and although we could spend time listing all the surprise offenders (looking at you, Canadian Prime Minister Justin Trudeau), the more important point is that *this* is why you always need to know the history before you borrow from black culture. You might think you're being a fan by repping Beyoncé's look for Halloween, but what your deep-bronzed face evokes for a lot of black folks is the spirit of Thomas Rice and his minstrel shows. (And just so we're clear, blackface is one of those cases where knowing the history still doesn't make it okay.)

The exchange of ideas, styles, and traditions is one of the tenets of a modern multicultural society. It's a part of how we grow, learn, advance. But cultural appropriation is something else. Cultural appropriation happens when members of a dominant group—in the United States, white people—take elements from the culture of a people who are disempowered. It's problematic for a number of reasons. For one, it trivializes historic oppression. It also lets people show love for a culture while still remaining prejudiced toward the people *of* that culture, and lets privileged people profit from the labor of oppressed people. On top of that, it can perpetuate racist stereotypes.

Let's dig into some more examples. Think of the trailblazing entertainer Little Richard, a black man who invented rock and roll, and Elvis being considered the "king" of it. Think of jazz developing in the black community and white saxophonist Kenny G being maybe the most famous contemporary jazz artist. Think of hip-hop's birth in the Bronx, an art form meant to draw attention to the struggle of people of color, and yet years later the highest-selling rap artist of all time is Eminem.

Are you still not convinced that cultural appropriation is everywhere? Let me point to actress Blake Lively flaunting her curves at a fancy film festival in Cannes, France, one year with the Instagram caption, "L.A. face with an Oakland booty." The statement was a nod to the popular 1990s song "Baby Got Back" by rapper Sir Mix-a-Lot. Widely popular from the moment it dropped, the megahit was a celebration of the curves of black women. Many saw Lively's comments as appropriating a song that was about and featured black women. Remember the phrase "Black is beautiful" that popped up in the 1970s? After centuries of being treated as "less than," black people worked hard to change that perception across the world. Seeing something created to affirm the beauty of black women, even a song like "Baby Got Back," rubbed people the wrong way. Take the Washington Redskins (Note: *redskin* is a racial slur used to disrespect Native Americans) keeping their culturally insensitive team name all the way to 2020. Or the Cleveland Indians, who for decades used an offensive, cartoonish picture of a Native American with an oversize smile as their team logo and mascot. Shout-out to both teams for, as of 2020, finally dropping the racist symbols, mascots, and names tied to their teams. Sports is a biggie, but major fashion brands like Gucci, Prada, and Burberry have been offenders, too. See high-end fashion brand Gucci selling a headscarf called the "Indy Full Turban." See Prada selling a key chain with a blackface caricature. See a model for Burberry strutting down the runway sporting a noose. Yes, a noose!

Some people have gone so far in their appropriation as to use chopsticks as a hair accessory. Just so we're all clear, Asian chopsticks are *not* the same as hair sticks. Using chopsticks to hold together your updo is the equivalent of sticking a fork in your hair. Gross.

And on and on.

LET'S GET UNCOMFORTABLE

Cultural appropriation is always an uncomfortable conversation. Think of how long black people have been demeaned in America. Think of how long their speech, their bodies, their skin color, their culture have been seen as lesser-than. Now imagine how hurtful it would be to have those same characteristics taken on by white people and celebrated as their own.

Conversations must be had about what is and isn't cultural appropriation, about the history of what is being appropriated, about how it makes people who have long been disenfranchised feel.

Call me biased, but we do have a lot of the coolest music, the best looks, the baddest athletes. Taking the brag down a notch, we have brilliant, creative people in every realm of American life who have been doing brilliant, creative work for generations, because of course we do. The goal of sounding the alarm about cultural appropriation is not to stop anyone, white people included, from celebrating black culture. The key is to celebrate it *as black culture*—not to take it as your own. The discomfort comes in the gray areas, I know. Just trust me that asking more questions, doing more homework, is better than maybe-plagiarizing any day.

TALK IT, WALK IT

If you're interested in aspects of a culture that is not your own—donning their hairstyles, wearing their fashion, listening to their music, reading literature by people of color, or watching movies grounded in another culture—you should do your homework. Find out about the genesis of the culture you want to engage with. If you want to wear braids, fine. But research where they came from. Be able to talk about it. I'm not saying everybody needs to become a historian, but if you're unsure about whether to engage with an aspect of black culture, talk about it with people who are informed. Yes, it might be uncomfortable, but there's a strong chance it will also be enlightening.

A few notes for the road. Once again, blackface is never okay, no reason, not ever. And while we're at it, don't do yellowface, brownface, or redface. Asians, Latinos, and Native Americans have also been hurt by people making caricatures of them by putting on makeup and exaggerating their speaking and physical features for "fun" and profit. Steer clear of adopting any ethnic stereotype: We could go through specifics all day, but basically, if whatever vibe you're going for relies on evoking a race that is not your own, don't. If you want to celebrate a holiday from a diverse culture, first do your homework. Don't pretend to be Mexican for Cinco de Mayo and think you're respecting the culture. It doesn't work that way. And please think *extra* hard about adapting sacred cultural artifacts. No wampum belts or Sikh turbans for either of us, please. Finally, make a point to engage with cultures on more than an aesthetic level. If the first goal here is to stop being ignorant, the second goal is just to learn more about one another. And that can be a lot of fun.

"I have unfortunately encountered many black people who seem hell-bent on hanging the history of slavery and racism and inequality around every single white person's neck. Who are unwilling to give grace if we ask questions to try to understand how we can be better. They are angry, and I'm not saying it isn't justified—anger is a form of grief, and it's allowed to a degree within the law. But if we all genuinely want to move forward, this is an obvious problem."

THE MYTHICAL ME

Angry Black Men

> To be a Negro in this country
> and to be relatively conscious is to
> be in a rage almost all the time.
>
> —JAMES BALDWIN

In Laurie Cassidy's article "The Myth of the Dangerous Black Man," she invites her reader into a thought experiment. Imagine yourself walking down a dark city street at night, she writes, and encountering a trio of young black men. She goes on:

> *What do you do as these young black men*
> *approach? How do you feel as they walk*
> *by on the sidewalk? What do you do as*

> *they pass you? . . . How do you see these*
> *three young men in dress, appearance,*
> *and demeanor? If you are a white per-*
> *son reading these lines, ask yourself if you*
> *would feel apprehensive or frightened?*
> *Do you make eye contact and say "hello,"*
> *or do you keep your eyes focused on the*
> *ground? Do you imagine that they are*
> *carrying weapons? Are you afraid that*
> *they might mug you? And do you feel*
> *guilty that you even feel this way? After*
> *seeing these young men do you feel more*
> *vulnerable to physical harm and are you*
> *more alert to your surroundings?*

Cassidy, who identifies herself as a middle-aged white woman, admits that she'd be "apprehensive" in the above scenario. But she also critiques her reaction, admitting that her response would not be based on actual experience with young black men, rather on ideas she's learned about them. While Cassidy uses the word *learned*, I'd take it a step further and call those ideas *indoctrination*. Indoctrination is what happens when someone is taught and fully accepts the ideas, opinions, and beliefs about a particular group without weighing other viewpoints about that same group. That's how implicit bias works.

Biases are absorbed, and instead of being educated away, they are reinforced. They turn into stereotypes that make it harder for every black person and other people of color to live a life free of racism. And none of these stereotypes are more pervasive, and more harmful, than the myth of the Angry Black Man.

Have you heard of it? Or can you remember what you did in a situation like the one Cassidy describes? How would you answer the same questions that she posed to herself?

LET'S REWIND

To understand the Angry Black Man stereotype and why it's so harmful, we have to take a trip in the way-back machine to 1915. By this time, black people had been legally free from enslavement for fifty years thanks to the Civil War and the passing of the Thirteenth Amendment. Two other amendments to our Constitution, the Fourteenth and Fifteenth, made black people U.S. citizens and gave black men the right to vote, respectively. Things appear to be looking up for black folks, right?

Ah, no. In fact, by 1915, black Americans had been stripped of many of the gains they made during Reconstruction—the short-lived period of racial progress made right after the Civil War. During Reconstruction, several black men were elected to local, state, and national office. Afraid of losing their grip on power, white people used laws, violence, and downright dirty lies to regain control over black people. One of the most enduring lies white people ever told about black people is that black men are predators out to harm white people. This myth is the granddaddy of the Angry Black Man myth. And D. W. Griffith made a fortune from this lie by using one of the newest inventions of his day—film—to launch one of the world's most dangerous and long-lasting slander campaigns.

Enter Griffith's film, the world's first blockbuster hit, *The Birth of a Nation*. Imagine being a kid in 1915 and going to a movie theater to watch the most anticipated film of the summer. You take your seat and begin shoving handfuls of popcorn into your mouth as the lights go down and the film begins to roll.

The movie is a reimagining of the Civil War and the period after it, Reconstruction. As the film rolls along, you notice that the main black male characters are actually played by white men wearing blackface. Even more shocking, those characters also happen to be the movie's primary villains. They are overly aggressive menaces and downright threatening, especially toward white women. At one point in the movie, a "black" man—played by a white dude in blackface—proposes marriage to a white woman. She's so distraught over the idea that she runs and jumps off a cliff. Triumphant music swells (it was the first movie ever to have a full orchestral score), and the audience breaks into applause. That's right. People all around you are clapping because the white woman in the movie would rather die than marry a black man. What do you think their reaction and this film teaches you to believe about black men?

The Birth of a Nation was a huge success. Then-president Woodrow Wilson screened it at the White House and is said to have commented, "It is like writing history with lightning. And my only regret is that it is all so terribly true." In fact, the daring nature of the film rocked the country. Not only did it strengthen racist ideas about black men across the fruited plain, it did so using cutting-edge film techniques like close-ups and epic battles, ensuring it would also be a film people talked about for decades to come. Filmmakers and moviegoers in other parts of the world watched the film, picking up new film skills as well as infectious racist ideas.

The Birth of a Nation also inspired the rebirth of the

Ku Klux Klan—a murderous white supremacist terror group. In the film, members of the KKK are depicted as heroes, riding in like the cavalry to protect Southern whites, white women in particular, from the clutches of menacing black men. Many white people believed this myth. The murderous practice of lynching often had at its heart the goal of protecting the chastity of white women, or so white men claimed. Remember Emmett Till. The fourteen-year-old teenager was brutally murdered by two white men in 1955 after he was accused of whistling at a white woman. Decades later, the white woman that accused him, Carolyn Bryant Donham, admitted that Till never touched, threatened, or harassed her. She had lied. And for that lie, Till, sadly, like so many black men before him, paid with his life. This myth was used as a convenient excuse to harm any black man or black neighborhood white people deemed "too uppity" (i.e., successful) for their comfort.

Take the town of Greenwood, in Tulsa, Oklahoma,

for example. In 1921, it was a prosperous all-black town, complete with its own bank, half a dozen fire departments, a movie theater, and rows of 1,200 nice homes. The town was so wealthy, it earned the name *Black Wall Street*. Greenwood owed its wealth to the discovery of oil on land that, twenty years earlier, was deemed undesirable. White people in neighboring towns grumbled over Greenwood's success. Those grumblings became a declaration of all-out war on May 31, 1921.

It all started when a black teen named Dick Rowland entered an elevator in Tulsa. Minutes later, the white woman working the elevator screamed, and Rowland fled. He was arrested the next day for assaulting her. A mob of angry white people showed up at the jail demanding that Rowland be released to them, while a posse of armed black people showed up to protect Rowland from what was sure to be a lynching. You can bet the black people who showed up to save Rowland were tired of being demonized as angry and dangerous despite their wealth and influence, tired of being at the mercy of white rage and ignorance.

Within hours, hundreds of armed white men stormed the town. Many of them had been given weapons and deputized by local officials (i.e., the folks in charge of *protecting* the city). Black men armed themselves as best they could to defend their families and their property. But the white mob had help—from above. A surviving eyewitness account from Buck Colbert Franklin, grandfather to the famed black historian John Hope Franklin, bears witness to the deadly attack that thundered down onto the helpless town:

> *I could see planes circling in mid-air. They grew in number and hummed, darted and dipped low. I could hear something like hail falling upon the top of my office building. Down East Archer, I saw the old Mid-Way hotel on fire, burning from its top, then another and another and another building began to burn from their top.*

Franklin was describing how the booming oil town was set on fire from above. Franklin continues:

> *Lurid flames roared and belched and licked their forked tongues into the air. Smoke ascended the sky in thick, black volumes and amid it all, the planes— now a dozen or more in number—still hummed and darted here and there with the agility of natural birds of the air.*

Outside his office, Franklin discovered how the planes managed to burn so many buildings: "The sidewalks were literally covered with burning turpentine balls. I knew all too well where they came from, and I knew all too well why every burning building first caught fire from the top." White men had flown over the city and tossed down what was the equivalent of Molotov cocktails (homemade bombs) to set Greenwood on fire.

For two days, Black Wall Street burned until most of it was ashes. And as it burned, the white mob shot and killed and abused black men, women, and children. By some historians' accounts, at least three hundred black people lost their lives during those fateful two days.

I wish I could tell you that scenes like Tulsa never happened again. But they did. Black towns being razed to the ground by angry white mobs wasn't uncommon at all.

Though, as with many myths, the Angry Black Man has a kernel of truth to it. *Not* the systematic assault on white women—the anger. In the time of slavery, black men, women, and children were regularly abused by white people. Now, imagine you were a black man, a father, and a husband, and you had to watch your loved ones be brutally treated by a white master or overseer. Day in and day out. White men and women even had the authority to sell your children or your wife away from you. And there was nothing you could do about it. Try to imagine the kind of hurt and anger you'd feel if this happened to you or to your children. And this would go on for generations.

Added to this agony is the reality that at any moment, your life, and the lives of your loved ones, can be taken by white mobs for almost any trumped-up reason. Especially if you are accused of touching, disrespecting, harassing, or harming a white woman.

Let's bring it back to the present. These destructive stereotypes and perceptions about black people are still alive and well in America and still threaten the lives of black people even today. Those intent on doing black people harm weaponize these stereotypes by in turn "weaponizing whiteness." We've already seen an example of this, with the murder of fourteen-year-old Emmett Till. More recently, you may have heard of Karen, or rather, Amy Cooper, who, on May 25, 2020, called the cops on a bird-watcher in Central Park because he wanted her to leash her illegally unleashed dog.

When Amy Cooper dialed 911, she used three words that are almost a death sentence to black men: "There's a black man who's *threatening my life*." That was a lie, and thank goodness the bird-watcher had the video receipts. She's also Jennifer Schulte, dubbed "Barbecue Becky," who called the police on two black men legally barbecuing in an Oakland park. "I'm really scared. Come quick," she said, code for "Do harm to these black men." And she is Alison Ettel, dubbed "Permit Patty," who called the police on an eight-year-old black girl selling water in San Francisco without a license. "I need to see your permit," she said. More recently, Miya Ponsetto attacked a fourteen-year-old black teen and falsely accused him of stealing her phone in a New York City hotel. She stated, "Take the case off—that's literally mine" and "No! I'm not letting him walk away with my phone!" as she attacked him trying to get "her phone" back.

Names aside, they're all Karen, the meme: an

entitled white woman who throws tantrums, asks to speak to the manager, and sometimes calls for the cavalry against a supposed angry black man. Karen is also the granddaughter of a much older figure, "Miss Ann." Miss Ann was the name enslaved black people gave to white mistresses who exerted power over them on the plantations. That's right—not only is there a long history of white women using their whiteness as a tool of control, there's a long history of meme-ing it. Even back then, black folks were paying attention. They had to if they hoped to survive and overcome their oppression.

This brings us back to James Baldwin's quote at the beginning of this chapter. Baldwin was a social activist and one of the twentieth century's most brilliant writers and thinkers. He grew up in the South and witnessed the violent swirl of rage and grief and hope that eventually morphed into the civil rights movement. Baldwin realized that any black person who was paying even the least bit of attention knew that white supremacy crippled black people in every way possible. So yes, black men were angry. Angry at the system of white supremacy that didn't protect black people and then punished them for protecting themselves.

Bring it back up to the present, and this is what makes a George Floyd possible, a Trayvon Martin—anytime someone has been seen as a threat because they've first been seen as black. There's a video that's shown up on my social media feeds a few times. The video shows a white guy named Jerry who is resisting arrest by two cops. Jerry wrestles with the two officers, manages to grab one of their batons, and beats one of them with it. Meanwhile, someone outside the frame can be heard saying, "Jerry, they're gonna hurt you . . . Jerry, don't do it." Jerry isn't hearing it, though. After huffing a moment, he proceeds to jump in the officers' car and drive off.

I invite you to pause here and think of all the times you've seen or read about police shooting a black man for much less. I invite you to read up on the death of Rayshard Brooks. Brooks was drunk, but he was the most calm, respectful drunk I've ever heard of. He was trying to de-escalate the conflict with an arresting officer. Then while he ran away with a Taser that no longer worked, Atlanta PD officer Garrett Rolfe shot him twice in the back.

Let's compare: Both Rayshard and Jerry resisted arrest. Only one of them beat the police with their own weapon, then stole their car and sped off. And only the other one died.

LET'S GET UNCOMFORTABLE

Like I said, in many cases, the anger of the black man is justified, if not for an immediate offense, then for the long train of historic offenses. It's not white people's job to police the feelings of black people, but as fellow human beings, please grant black people the right to the full spectrum of emotions regarding their wounds.

You've likely heard of Karen and recognized the name as derogatory. And there's a good chance you've seen a version of an angry black man in the media. The memes, the images, the art . . . they are all political. Where do these stereotypes come from? Who do these stereotypes serve? In what ways, if any, have you perpetuated them? If you've found yourself upset by Karen becoming a meme, ask yourself if you're looking at her in the fullest historical and cultural context. Ask yourself if you're equally disturbed by the myth of the angry black man and what's happened to both of them as a result of that myth.

In the opening of this chapter, I talked about Laurie Cassidy's article "The Myth of the Dangerous Black Man" and how she recognized that her feeling threatened by black men was unjustified. That's a good place for anyone to start.

TALK IT, WALK IT

You may be wondering by now: Am I angry?

Sometimes. Just like you are.

What you can do right now is start paying attention to how many times white people weaponize their whiteness against black people and to how many times the myth of the angry black man leads to violence against one of them. If you are a white woman, please don't be a Karen. If you're a white man, please don't be a white man with a gun pointed at my brother.

I also invite you all to read *Stamped: Racism, Antiracism, and You* by Ibram X. Kendi and Jason Reynolds or *Dark Sky Rising: Reconstruction and the Dawn of Jim Crow* by Henry Louis Gates Jr. and Tonya Bolden, and share *Antiracist Baby* by Ibram X. Kendi and Ashley Lukashevsky with your younger siblings. We got to start the youngins out right. Before I close, I want to leave you with this: If you see a black man and he is angry, obviously don't assume he's angry because he's black, but also don't assume he's even angry at anything racism-related in that moment. Let people have emotions. See him as an individual.

"*If the N word is such a bad word,
why do my black friends use it all the
time towards each other?*"

NOOOOOPE!

The N-Word

We have a #$%&er in the whitehouse.

—BUCK BURNETTE

I was seventeen years old, just a kid, for part of my freshman year at the University of Texas in 2008. That year was notable, not just for being my freshman year but because Barack Hussein Obama II—shout-out to Kenya—got elected president. Well, that same year, when I was a bushy-tailed and bright-eyed freshman football player at the University of Texas, I was teammates with a guy named Buck Burnette, a backup center (the guy that stands under the quarterback on offense). Not too long after President Obama was elected, old Buck updated his profile with the following message: "All the hunters gather up, we have a #$%&er in the whitehouse." That post got Buck kicked off the team quick, and it's a good thing it did. Keep in mind, on your average college football team, there are about eighty black people. And almost all eighty of those guys on the team that year were ready to find Buck and throw hands. To this day, I've never seen Buck again. I think he issued an apology. But our head coach, Mack Brown, still found it unacceptable. That story about Buck is a kind of long-winded way of saying something that's pretty simple: Don't use the N-word. Ever. As in, under no circumstances should you use it. The N-word is forever off-limits. And that includes writing it with symbols.

Imagine the worst insult you've ever received. Now imagine that when you heard those words, what you also heard was that you're second-class forever. That you don't deserve any of this American dream. Imagine what you heard was, *You're an animal.* Imagine you heard, *You're stupid. You're a slave. My people owned your people, and you were better off when they did.* Imagine that you heard, *You won't amount to anything, boy. And the nothing you get is exactly what you deserve.* If you can picture one word communicating all of that, then you'll have some sense of what hearing the N-word does to me and any other black person in America.

LET'S REWIND

We can trace the word all the way back to the Latin *niger*, which simply meant *black*. This became *Negro* in the Americas when colonist John Rolfe (the guy who married a native woman who is widely known today by what was her nickname, *Pocahontas* (yes, like the Disney movie)) wrote a letter to a British official describing the arrival of "20 and odd Negroes" in the Jamestown colony of Virginia. In 1775, the first offensive use of the N-word shows up—and boy, did that catch on. By the 1800s, the term had entered the

American vocabulary, and from the eighteenth century on, use of the word and its related imagery exploded. The N-word, alongside offensive images of black people, started showing up on cigarette boxes, on food packaging, on TV and movie screens, in books, in music, in lily-white neighborhoods. Remember this counting game: "Eeny, meeny, miny, moe, catch a tiger by his toe. If he hollers let him go"? Well, there was a time when that toe didn't belong to a tiger. All with the express purpose of demeaning black people.

The word fell out of favor and widespread usage by black people during the time of the civil rights movement, thanks in no small part to thinkers like James Baldwin: "We have invented the nigger. I didn't invent him. White people invented him," Baldwin said. "I've known and I've always known . . . that I'm not a nigger." Yet the term got picked up again as hip-hop became a cultural juggernaut in the late 1980s. Years before Ice Cube was a family-friendly addition to movies like *Are We There Yet?* or *Ride Along*, he was a scowling member of the late 1980s Compton rap group named N.W.A: Niggaz Wit Attitudes. From the height of the group's early 1990s popularity till now, the word *nigga* has been a staple in rap lyrics.

Niger, N-word, nigga. The last version is the form of the word that black people have used to seize some of the power over the word, to turn something that was meant to harm us into something that might just have the potential to heal us. *Nigga* is a term of endearment between some black people—the softening of the hard *ER* is key, as is the fact that it's reserved for intimate, black-to-black exchanges. It's a way for black people to commune, to create a space that's only for us. It is not, like any of the other forms of the word, a word that is available to white people.

This usage is not without its detractors. Poet Maya Angelou once said, "The N-word was created to divest people of their humanity. When I see a bottle [and] it says 'P-O-I-S-O-N' then I know [what it is]. The bottle is nothing, but the content is poison.

If I pour that content into Bavarian crystal, it is still poison." This was Angelou's response to those black people, like Ice Cube, who had reappropriated and assimilated the word. She thought that there was no softening or sanitizing or transmuting the N-word, even for our people.

In a move aligned with Angelou's thinking, the NAACP held a funeral for the word in Detroit. That 2007 ceremony included two Percheron horses, a pine box adorned with a bouquet of fake black roses and a black ribbon, and white-gloved pallbearers. The ceremony was presided over by then Detroit mayor Kwame Kilpatrick. "Today we're not just burying the N-word, we're taking it out of our spirit," said Kilpatrick. "We gather burying all the things that go with the N-word."

Kilpatrick and the NAACP didn't succeed in banishing/burying the N-word. Four hundred years later, it's still the most infamous word in American culture. And many black people still argue that using *nigga* or *niggah* or other forms of the word is, instead of poison, a way to empty the word of some of its original hatred. What's more popular in American culture than hip-hop, where *nigga* has been very much alive and well since the days of N.W.A? Kendrick Lamar's hit "Alright" begins, "All my life I had to fight, nigga," and features a chorus of "Nigga, we gon' be alright Huh? / We gon' be alright Nigga, we gon' be alright."

If black people do or don't say it, that's our choice. Either way, unfortunately, there will always be white people, white men especially (a group that should be the very last on earth to even consider using it) who feel entitled enough to use the word.

LET'S GET UNCOMFORTABLE

Last year, controversy erupted on social media after Puerto Rican actress Gina Rodriguez posted an IG vid of herself rapping the classic Fugees hit "Ready or Not," N-word included.

During an interview on the radio show *The*

Breakfast Club, Trevor Noah, comedian and host of *The Daily Show*, had something to say on why non-black people using the N-word is a no-go.

"In America," he said, "there's a fundamental confusion that happens in and around hip-hop, and some people don't understand the sensitivities that they need to have in and around words that they use . . . Some people need to say to themselves, 'I grew up with hip-hop. I may have identified with black culture. But I also understand that I'm not black or I have not lived the black experience.'"

Then Noah joked, "As black people, it's like the one perk to the oppression is getting the N-word in a weird way."

When one of the radio show's hosts added that sometimes people say they get caught up in the moment as they sing their favorite songs and can't avoid saying the N-word (assumedly like Gina Rodriguez, who started that week's N-word storm), Noah wasn't having it.

"Everyone knows how to censor themselves," he said.

Noah finished the conversation by adding, "I know that it's black people who should be deciding the thing [about who can or cannot say the N-word] ... But if you are not black, I can save you a lot of stress in your life by just saying don't do it."

Hopefully more folks are getting the message. A day after dropping the N-word bomb, Gina Rodriguez posted an apology, saying, "The word I sang carries with it a legacy of hurt and pain that I cannot even imagine ... I have some serious learning and growing to do and I am so deeply sorry for the pain I have caused."

Now, remember words do not have meaning without context. You might call your girlfriend or boyfriend "babe" or "baby" or other sweet nothings, because there is an established relationship between the two of you. I have a friend who's a rapper who calls his wife "fat." Fellas, I don't recommend trying this one, but it works for him and his relationship. I wouldn't dare tell him what he should call his wife, because their relationship and bond is theirs and theirs only. No one can or should tell you what you can call someone with whom you have an established relationship that they are not privy to. The same goes for the word *nigga* among the black community. There is an established relationship with most black people (not all tolerate the word) where we have decided that it is okay to call each other nigga. No one should attempt to tell black people otherwise.

Once again, there is no conversation that excuses a non-black person using the N-word. There's too much pain in that word coming from a non-black mouth. However, I will also say that if you're ever inclined to use it, you can and should investigate why you want to use it. That's the difficult conversation, not *if* you should or shouldn't say it but *why* you want to say it at all. If the N-word is in your heart or on your tongue, please, please try to figure out why.

TALK IT, WALK IT

After Buck Burnette's Facebook post went public, he deleted his Facebook account, though it didn't matter much, since he was already national news. Before he did, though, he posted a half-contrite apology to his page:

> *Clearly I have made a mistake and apologized for it and will pay for it. I received it as a text message from an acquaintance and immaturely put it up on facebook in the light of the election. Im not racist and apologize for offending you. I grew up on a ranch in a small town where that was a real thing and I need to grow up. I sincerely am sorry for being ignorant in thinking that it would be ok to write that publicly and apologize to you in particular. I have to be more mature than to put the reputation of my team at stake and to spread that kind of hate which I dont even believe in. Once again, I sincerely apologize.*
> (Quote not edited for typos)

It seems that Buck's initial takeaway was as much that he'd made the mistake of posting his feelings publicly as it was that his sentiments were wrong in and of themselves. And he must've got some schooling on his position, because the published apology he made later to the Associated Press was a bit more polished: "The lack of judgment on my part has had devastating consequences," said Buck. "Those that know me understand that this is not a true reflection of my character. I sincerely apologize to everyone that I have offended. I have had the opportunity to apologize to my teammates and coaches and have received support from many of them in return."

Let's hope you won't need to make any private or public apologies for using the N-word. As always, continue to try to reflect critically on how you use language and the extent to which language reflects your innermost thoughts and feelings. If you can't help yourself, I suggest you stop rapping along to the music.

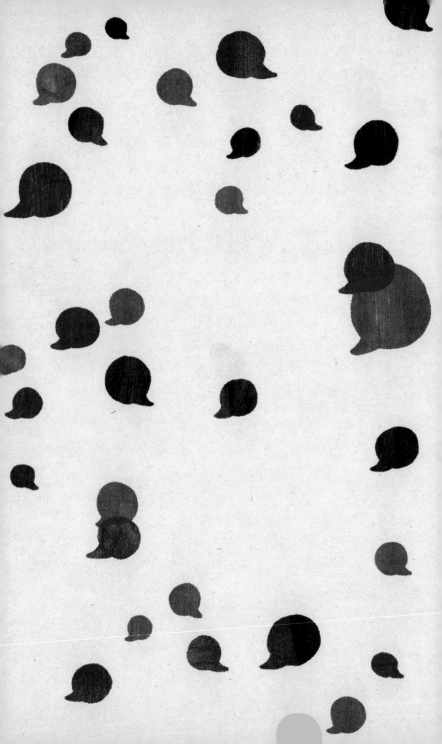

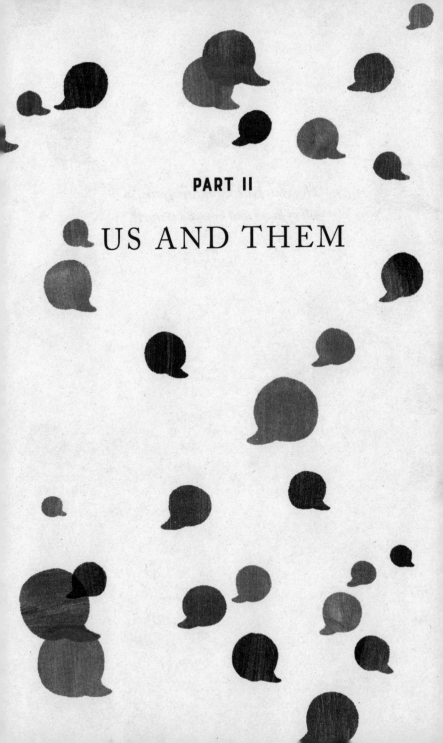

PART II

US AND THEM

"How has systemic racism gotten so out of hand and how did it start?"

THE GAME IS RIGGED

Systemic Racism

That dream of a land in which life
should be better and richer and fuller
for everyone, with opportunity for each
according to ability or achievement.

—JAMES TRUSLOW ADAMS,
The Epic of America (1831), coining the term American dream

Young peoples, a heads-up: Before I get into the chapter, I want to let you know this one and the next might be a little tougher to wrap your heads around at first. They both feature big concepts (and maybe a greater than average amount of big words) that have long histories and implicate a lot of people. But trust me when I tell you the chapters are necessary. They will pay off. And even if you don't realize the payoff in the short run, just wait, 'cause there's always the long run. It's greater later, as they sometimes say.

Now that I've given you the heads-up, let me tell you about this time months ago, when I visited a white friend who'd just moved into a new house in Austin, Texas. It was a super nice place: four bedrooms, huge space. I could tell how proud he was as he showed me around. Then in the midst of the tour, he said, "Bro, check out these windows. They came with these plantation shutters."

It was like the record scratched on the happy soundtrack of the tour. I cringed. Good friend that he was, he saw my reaction and apologized. But the whole rest of the tour, and the rest of the day, I was thinking, *Why in the heck do we still have things called plantation shutters?* Young brothers and sisters, you may be thinking, *Why is he buggin' over plantation shutters?* It's because plantations are a reminder of the worst thing America has ever done, and thousands of Americans are still raking in the dough by selling an approximation of the "authentic" plantation experience.

Even now, I can't help but wonder why we still have plantations at all in this country. They've been romanticized to the point where folks hold weddings, work conferences, and weekend getaways on plantations that once held twelve generations of humans in bondage. People pay good money for guided tours, admiring the architecture and history from a (thankfully) long-gone way of life. All of this while ignoring the wretched history of slavery and the atrocities that took place on plantations.

And don't even get me started on the Confederate flag, which I'm sure waves proudly over some of those plantation destination spots. If there is a more deeply offensive symbol of racism and hate than plantations, it is the Confederate flag. Some people have argued that this flag was used by the Confederate army during the Civil War to symbolize states' rights.

I was even taught that in some classes growing up, and while that may be accurate, it is incomplete. Yet, those who proudly fly it today (at least one of whom took part in the Capitol Hill insurrection) still argue it's meant to show pride for Southern heritage. Let's sit on these arguments for a sec.

First, what right did the Confederate, slaveholding Southern states want to keep so badly that they were willing to go to war for it? You've got it—the right to own and sell and dehumanize other human beings. And because the Civil War was started over slavery (yes, it was, and don't let anyone tell you differently) by those Southern states that cherished their right to enslave and demean black people so much they were willing to *form their own country* to do it, you have to assume that the pride this flag supposedly symbolizes is born out of rebellion, treason, and hatred. Still not convinced? Consider that the Confederate flag, in the years following the Civil War, continued to be used by segregation-loving white Americans and murderous anti-black hate groups like the Ku Klux Klan.

These symbols are powerful reminders of America's racist history. The plantation is a symbol of the bondage black people suffered. The Confederate flag is a symbol of the system of laws and racist beliefs that made that bondage possible in the first place. Because, get this fam, slavery and segregation could not have lasted for nearly four hundred years unless there was a system—meaning, the set way things work together to support the whole body—in place to enforce it. And because that system has lasted for so long, it's become ingrained in every part of our country—our laws, entertainment, the books we read, the prison system, where people can live and not live, healthcare, even how long a person can expect to live . . . and on and on and on. And something else—once racism infects a system, it self-replicates, like cancer, becomes something almost impossible to remove.

It's not always obvious, but don't ever let anyone convince you that we are in a racism-free or, as some folks like to say, a "post-racial America." This term got thrown around a lot between 2008 and 2016 when many people thought, with a black president, how could America possibly still be racist? You don't hear the phrase so much anymore. But let me be clear: We will never achieve a post-racial America as long as the levers of systemic racism continue to churn.

After all, even though American slavery ended in 1865, racism in many forms, including segregation laws, reigned supreme for another hundred years. When you total the number of years of legalized racism and legalized racist practices, from when the first enslaved people landed here in 1619 until the end of the civil rights movement in 1968, that's 349 years of government-approved hate and racism. Now compare that figure to the number of years between 1968 and the year this book was published, 2021. That's 53 years. Yeah, America's been okay with racist policies, laws, and practices for a *lot* longer than overt racism has been illegal. Think about it. For over four hundred years, racism has been soaking into the soil of our nation—from the colonial years to the present.

In 1931, historian James Truslow Adams coined the term *American dream.* I'm sure we can all agree that an America built on "opportunity for each according to ability or achievement" sounds like a pretty great place to live. But it's a place that America has never been—especially for black people. We've already seen how the dream gets deferred on the individual level, in the everyday interactions between black and white Americans: through implicit bias, white privilege, and cultural appropriation; through harmful stereotypes and punishing language.

Those everyday traces are the fingerprints of an even bigger, more deeply entrenched reality. (Here's your warning to strap in—this section of the book is gonna be a bumpy ride.) If you want to know the major reason America hasn't lived up to the stated ideals of its Founding Fathers and of Mr. James Truslow Adams, it's due to a little thing called systemic (or structural or institutional) racism.

I'll be the first to admit that *systemic racism* sounds like a conspiracy. But guess what? If there is anything in America that fits the definition of a national conspiracy, it's systemic or structural racism. Racism is a form of oppression, a.k.a. those with more power putting their thumb on those with less power. And oppression is as old as civilization. Search as far back as you like: As soon as a group of people start creating rules for themselves, as soon as they start divvying up power, customs, a government—somebody is going to get oppressed. Sooner or later, there will be systems in place to ensure that some people fare better than others. In America, like many other countries founded on colonialism (even before we get to slavery!), the rule-makers were white, and those faring worse are black and brown people. Colonialism was the result of powerful European countries invading foreign lands and claiming those lands for themselves. They destroyed existing cultures and kingdoms, then planted new colonies and nations on top of them. All the time, the colonizers took resources from those lands and forced the original inhabitants to recognize them as their rulers. For example, North America was once home to hundreds of thousands of Native Americans; each one was a member of a native nation. When European colonizers (ahem, "explorers") arrived on the continent, they used shady contracts, unfair laws, and violence to forcibly take land from the indigenous peoples. After the United States of America was formed and the colonial era was over, our government continued this cycle of deceit, illegal acts, and violence against native people for centuries.

Spoiler alert: A lot of those systems are still chugging along today.

William Faulkner once wrote, "The past is never dead. It's not even past." Think about my friend's plantation shutters: the history of slavery literally hanging in plain sight. Think about Mississippi waiting until July of 2020 to remove *the literal Confederate flag* from its state flag. An evil, oppressive past is right here with us. And it's not hiding in plain sight. It's raising its arms and saying, "LOOK!"

LET'S REWIND

It's tough to talk about systemic racism without sounding like a professor, so cut me a little slack for a couple of paragraphs. For starters, a definition: *systemic racism* is every dynamic—historic, cultural, political, economic, institutional, and person-to-person—that gives advantages to white people, while at the same time producing a whole host of terrible effects for black people and other people of color. Those effects show up as inequalities in every part of our lives and in how we are treated by those in power. In criminal justice, black people are jailed at five times the rate of white people. In terms of power, there have been forty-six different presidents, and only one of them (President Barack Obama!) was not a white guy. And up until January of 2021 and the election of Kamala Harris, all of the vice presidents were white, too. And if that wasn't convincing enough, there have only been four black governors and ten black senators in the two-hundred-plus-year history of our nation's Congress. Which is to say systemic racism is making the unequal treatment of people of color the national norm.

I could spend the rest of this book detailing different parts of structural racism, but for now, I'll take on a few major areas: housing, schooling, and criminal justice. The racism ingrained in each of these areas of life perpetuates a vicious cycle in which certain groups, including black folks, are held down while other groups—namely, white folks—are elevated.

If you'll recall from the chapter on white privilege, black families have just one tenth the wealth of white families. A big reason for that is real estate. One of the most common ways to build wealth is to own a home in a desirable neighborhood. Over time, as the neighborhood grows better and stronger, the value of the home increases. When the home is sold, the owners can make a sizable profit and use that money to help buy a new home, put a child through college, pay other expenses, or save for future generations. For decades, there have been structural barriers in place to keep black people from reaping the benefits of owning a home. Back in 1934, a dude named Homer Hoyt, then the chief economist of the Federal Housing Authority (FHA), wrote a report to help his agency standardize home ownership loans in which he ranked various nationalities by order of "desirability." The most desired on the list were Anglo-Saxons and northern Europeans (this whole white race business was still coming together), and at the bottom of the list were Mexicans and "Negroes."

The FHA took this ranking and ran with it. They mapped out cities, dividing them into which neighborhoods were "riskier" to lend money to, with race being the most used factor for determining risk. Neighborhoods where the white Protestant (a denomination of Christianity) Anglo-Saxons lived were marked in green, and, with other colors representing other groups in between, the neighborhoods where black people and Mexicans lived were marked in red. This is where we get the term *redlining*, which forced tons of black people into doing business with deceptive lenders who gave them unfair terms for home mortgages in neighborhoods that were deemed "undesirable" and therefore less valuable than green—or rather white—neighborhoods.

Hoyt's thinking was written into a bunch of real estate practices, from biased rules of homeowners' associations to hair-trigger evictions. And while redlining was outlawed in 1968 with the Fair Housing Act, it's still in practice in plenty of ways today, shaping what neighborhoods look like all over America. Heck, according to a 2016 Pew Research Center study, only 43 percent of black households are home-owners, contrasted with nearly 72 percent of white households. Add to that statistic that homeownership is the most common way to create, build, and pass on wealth from one generation to the next, and you can begin to see how white families pass down advantages to their children, while black families aren't able to set up their kids for the future. And the cycle continues.

Our public school system is just as flawed, and for related reasons. In most states, school funding breaks down like this: state taxes (45 percent), local taxes (45 percent), and federal taxes (10 percent). While states sometimes provide extra funds for poorer school systems, it's not usually enough to level the playing field. If the homes in a school's neighborhood are worth less than the homes of schools in other neighborhoods, then those owners pay fewer taxes. If there are fewer businesses in the particular neighborhood, there will also be much less tax revenue. So schools in poor neighborhoods are forced to do more with less.

In other words, wealthier neighborhoods get more money to fund their schools, while schools in poorer neighborhoods have to make do with fewer state and local tax dollars. It all adds up to a system described by Pulitzer Prize–winning journalist Nikole Hannah-Jones as "separate and unequal."

And that's just the numbers. We also have to look at the history of the black community's relationship to schooling in this country. We can't lose sight of the truth that when black people were enslaved, they were forbidden to read and write, that their white owners did everything they could think of to keep them illiterate, undereducated, ignorant. Imagine what kind of effect that had on those enslaved people, on their children, and their children's children. You know how your parents and teachers force you to do summer reading (hopefully this isn't one of those required reading books), well yeah, it was the polar opposite of that for enslaved black people. For them, reading wasn't allowed. Here's a little more perspective.

Founded in 1636, Harvard is the oldest institution of higher learning in America. Harvard, like the vast majority of universities that would follow it until the 1950s–1970s, didn't allow black students to enroll. Havens of higher education for black people for over a century, historically black colleges and universities (HBCUs), were almost exclusively the only game in town for any black person looking to get a degree. The oldest HBCU is Cheyney University of Pennsylvania, founded in 1837. So there's a two-hundred-year gap of higher education between white and black people.

Black people have had to face numerous hardships because of that gap. Year after year, schools in poorer black neighborhoods are underfunded. Black students are taught a curriculum that rarely centers their culture, history, or experiences. These factors can make learning extremely difficult for black kids, leading some of them to believe their education doesn't matter. Time after time, research has shown that gaps between black and white students begin early in childhood and only widen with age. The socio-economic makeup of a school can play a larger role in achievement than the poverty of an individual student's family, and a poor education has a huge effect on later fortunes.

Then there is the possibility of jail or prison. Pick your stat: According to a 2012 Annie E. Casey Foundation study, a student not performing on grade level by the end of the third grade is four times less likely to graduate. According to a 2009 study by Northeastern University, high school dropouts are sixty-three times more likely to be incarcerated than college grads. There are a lot of reasons for these grim statistics, but you needn't be a mathematician to see a connection between schools and prisons. Social scientists call this relationship the *school-to-prison pipeline*.

Which finally brings me to the criminal justice system. As we saw earlier, studies have shown that white teachers are more likely to monitor and punish black children, particularly black boys, for negative behavior than white children. Black people are much more likely to become involved in the criminal justice system than white people. At about 13 percent of the U.S. population, black people make up more than 33 percent of those in federal and state prisons. That overrepresentation is not an accident but rather the product of systemic racism. Black people are not any more criminal than anyone else (more on that in chapter 10), but they've been criminalized as much or more than any group in America.

Ironically, some say this started with a little adjustment to the U.S. Constitution called the Thirteenth Amendment. This was the amendment, or change, added to the Constitution that made slavery illegal—with one glaring exception. It reads: "Neither slavery nor involuntary servitude, **except as a punishment for crime whereof the party shall have been duly convicted**, shall exist within the United States, or any place subject to their jurisdiction." Yeah, I bolded that clause for a reason. Plenty of scholars have linked that exception clause to the rise of what's now called *mass incarceration* or the *prison industrial complex*.

Now, why do scholars link mass incarceration today to a clause that was passed back in 1865—over 150 years ago? It's because this exception clause in the Thirteenth Amendment has been used to reintroduce slavery to America since its passage after the Civil War. Practices that forced black people to work against their will—like convict leasing and prison chain gangs. These practices were especially common in the South, where white people were horrified by the idea that people they had once owned were now their equals in the eyes of the law. Farms and plantations that were once worked by enslaved labor were now in dire need of workers. And the cheaper the labor, the better for white landowners. By making deals with local prisons, the landowners could "lease" jailed people, usually black males, to work for them. It wasn't that black people had all of a sudden become criminals; these men were often convicted of trumped-up crimes like walking beside a railroad or speaking too loudly around a white woman, and sentenced to several years of "hard labor." Almost overnight, jails that were previously filled with white males became overcrowded with black men. Convict leasing became so popular that a whole category of laws, *Black Codes*, and eventually *Pig Laws*, were created after the Civil War to make breathing while black as criminal as possible. To enforce Pig Laws (named such because of their association with livestock theft), some cities started police departments or gave local men (some of whom were former slave catchers) the authority to look out for black law breakers. These laws would eventually evolve into Jim Crow laws that upheld segregation in the South for a century.

While the Thirteenth Amendment ended slavery on the surface, its loophole paved the way for returning many black people to slavery.

Prisons today don't have programs like that. They just have mandatory labor projects—like fighting

dangerous forest fires in California, working plantations in Mississippi, or maintaining golf courses in
Georgia—without a living wage, done disproportionately by incarcerated black people. Hmm.

LET'S GET UNCOMFORTABLE

Okay. Deep breath. Systemic racism is hard to talk
about because it seems so big, so pervasive. And it is.
I've touched on a few of the places it rears its head,
but the truth is that it pervades almost *all* areas of
American life, and it's even harder to figure out what
role an individual white person plays in the system.

Let's address that last part head-on. Young white
brothers and sisters, I hear you. None of this is your
fault individually. And maybe you've traced your family tree back generations and found that neither your
great-great-great-grandparents nor anyone else in
your family owned slaves (prayer hands to that for
sure). But on the other hand, can you trace your family
tree as far back as it goes in America and claim that

every single person on your family tree was a staunch abolitionist? That every single one of them acknowledged all aspects of their white privilege and called out racism wherever it arose? That's a much harder project. That might well be an impossible one.

I hope you see where I'm going with this. Remember what I said about white privilege, how you don't even have to do anything to have it work for you? Well, it's worked that way for as long as it's been around, which means you've likely spent your whole life enjoying the fruits of systemic racism and without ever having to directly engage with its fallout.

Luckily, you're here now to engage and be a part of the solution.

TALK IT, WALK IT

No one can fight systemic racism alone. It's too big and in too many areas. On the flip side, that means there are a million ways to help.

As always, a good place to start is learning more.

Visit the We Need Diverse Books online (wndb.org) for excellent books on anti-racism and about people with diverse racial and ethnic backgrounds. The more we know about the historical and lived experiences of other groups, the easier it is for us to see systemic racism and fight it. At school, ask your administrators about hiring black teachers and other leaders of color to increase your school's diversity. Take political action whenever and wherever you can by volunteering your time to causes that matter to you and peacefully protesting when needed. Undoing systemic racism is nothing short of pulling apart white supremacy. It's going to take a herculean effort by all of us to tear it down.

"*I know you've suffered because of things you didn't do or couldn't control, but making me suffer just moves the problem instead of making it go away.*"

STANDING UP TO YOUR BULLIES

Reverse Racism

> To abandon affirmative action is
> to say there is nothing more to be
> done about discrimination.
>
> **—CORETTA SCOTT KING**

Before I get into this chapter, I want to stress something important, maybe the most important thing to understanding race in America. Here it is: Whiteness is everywhere.

It is the default setting, or the norm, in American life. Don't believe me? I'll prove it. Close your eyes. Now think about your favorite book. Picture the main character in that book. Now quick, tell me, what does that character look like? Is he or she white? Black? Asian? Latinx? Native American? If you said *white*, it's not surprising. In fact, as of 2018, over 50 percent of children's books published in America featured white characters. The next-largest main characters in children's books were animal or inanimate objects like toys or cars—27 percent. That means that 77 percent of all children's books published in 2018 did not feature black or POC kids as main characters. Books featuring black children were only 10 percent of the total. We've got a problem, America, when black children and other POC youth are more likely to pick up a book and see an animal or truck than themselves reflected back at them.

Young brothers and sisters, perhaps some of you can relate to what I'm about to share with you.

Like I've said, I went to private school from fifth

grade to twelfth grade. Well, at my school, there was a black kid in my class; his name was John Criss. Based on how the white kids at our school perceived blackness, a big part of which was by athletic standards, and also by how you looked and dressed, John looked the part. John was dark-skinned and wore cornrows or an Afro just about from the time we were in fifth grade to the time we were in twelfth grade. John ran track. He played football. He was a receiver on the football team. He played basketball, though he was not the greatest basketball player. He was relatively fast. But there was one thing—John was really, really good at math. Like nerdy good at math. Like always had a TI-84 Plus on him. Now I'm not saying that a black kid can't be good at math—clearly, John was a smart kid—but I am saying that there isn't really a popular idea of black kids being math whizzes. So John was really good at math, and to tell you the truth, he was kind of nerdy. And he alllllwaays got bullied, always. Bullied by the white kids at our school because he looked "blackety black," as the white kids would try to call it, and had cornrows and whatnot, but didn't carry himself like the white kids thought a black person should. For example, John wouldn't swag out his football jerseys. Instead, he'd tuck his shirt into his pants—would do it even when we weren't in uniform—and hike them up to his belly button. He was just kind of different from the rest of us, and so he was always getting bullied from both sides: the white people in school and the black. I'll never forget the time when people were going at John relentlessly in the gym, and he retaliated by saying, "Bone crusher. I ain't ever scared" (which is from an old rap song, by the way), and then people started mocking him even worse.

Now that we've expanded our definition of racism to include the systems that feed it, I'd like to address another supposed flavor: reverse racism, also known as the idea of black people (or anyone non-white) being racist against white people. I've had many people ask me if reverse racism exists. They often pair this with a second question: Is it even possible for black people to be racist?

The first thing to understand is that those are two very different questions. About the latter, I'll cite the answer Dr. Ibram X. Kendi, a historian and expert on racism, gave during a CNN interview last year:

> *You have black people who believe that they can't be racist because they believe that black people don't have power, and that's blatantly not true. Every single person on earth has the power to resist racist policies and power. We need to recognize that there are black people who resist it, and there are some who do not. And then you have black people, a limited number, who are in policy, making decisions to institute or defend policies that harm black people.*

So there you have it. One of America's foremost experts on racism, calling out the belief that black people can't be racist. But let me point out a couple of things. First, Dr. Kendi's claims concern black people being racist against other black people. This is a tragic set of beliefs called *internalized racism* that develops when members of an oppressed racial group adopt white supremacist ideas that lead them to hate or loathe themselves and others within their racial group. Second, when he is talking about black people in a position to make policy either for or against racism, note the key phrase: *a limited number.*

When I say that reverse racism is a myth, what I mean is that, while individual black people can be prejudiced against white people, reverse racism by black people against white people just doesn't exist. It can't exist, because that's not how collective power works in this country. In other words, in order to act, as a group, upon racist beliefs, you must have power over the group you want to oppress. Black people do not hold power over white people in this country.

They never have. No group in America holds power over white people.

What is reverse racism, if it's not, well, real? It's a prime example of what scholar Alice McIntyre calls *white talk*: a.k.a. strategies white people use—consciously or not—to insulate themselves from their collective participation in racism. Another way into this idea is the term *white fragility*, recently popularized by sociologist Robin DiAngelo. When white people are put in situations that make them uncomfortable and challenge their identity, "we withdraw, defend, cry, argue, minimize, ignore," explains DiAngelo. "And in other ways push back to regain our racial position and equilibrium." Put very simply—white folks get defensive. The feeling of defensiveness is white fragility, and the way they hit back, with accusations like reverse racism, is white talk.

I'll unpack more white talk below; some of it may be familiar to you. Stay with me. Keep your eyes and heart open.

LET'S REWIND

I repeat: There is no such thing as reverse racism. If you want to oppress someone, you're gonna need power over them as a group—and no group holds it over white people. There literally aren't enough black people with institutional authority over white people in America to facilitate systemic racism against them. On a purely numbers level, this would be tough: Black celebrities may loom large in our society, but black people are still only 13.4 percent of the population (whites still make up 59.7 percent). While whites are predicted to be a statistical minority in America by 2045, black people are a long, long ways off, if not forever, from dominating in this country.

And yet, white folks argue in favor of reverse racism every day. Calling back to cultural appropriation, some people think it's reverse racism to get criticism for wearing dreadlocks or for renaming traditional African hairstyles after a white woman. Others cry reverse racism for the forever ban on them using the N-word, especially if black people can use derogatory words for a white person (which I don't encourage) without the same backlash. But as I hope I've proven, these phony arguments are what I mean by *white talk*.

One of the most common examples of white talk is calling Affirmative Action reverse racism. To explain why that's wrong, I want to take us back to 1961, almost a hundred years after the Civil War, when President John F. Kennedy signed Executive Order (EO) 10925, which instructed federal contractors to take "affirmative action to ensure that job applicants are treated equally without regard to race, color, religion, sex, or national origin." That order was the nation's first instance of Affirmative Action. Since then, it's been implemented (and challenged) in a number of areas where systemic racism has persisted.

In a nutshell, Affirmative Action is an effort to make up for the systemic inequalities caused by centuries of discrimination. To achieve some measure of social equality, it gives special treatment to groups (POC and women) that have suffered those long-standing inequalities. Some people argue that it's unfair to now give black people preference over white people. To that, I say, "What's fair?" If you ask me, fairness can only occur between equal parties, and black people have never been treated as equals in America. As a matter of fact, unfairness doesn't even scratch the surface of how they've been treated. Let's sit on this point for a hot second. Folks who are against Affirmative Action say it's unfair because it doesn't treat all people exactly the same. They are ignoring the fact that for centuries, white people have benefited from laws and policies that have treated black people unequally. These people don't understand the difference between equity and equality. In order to get to a place in America where all people are truly equal, meaning each person or group of people is given the same resources or opportunities, we must first make up for past wrongs. This is where equity, treating people according to their circumstances, comes into play. Equity-based policies like Affirmative Action recognize that black people and white people have had vastly different circumstances in America and, in order to mend the wrongs in the past, black people (and other millions of POC hurt by racism) need additional resources and opportunities to close the gaps that centuries of oppression have created. Only after these gaps are closed can black people have true equality with white people.

"But *my* ancestors didn't own slaves," you may have heard. "Why should I be the one who doesn't get the job or the scholarship, who gets stuck on the waiting list?" Or "I grew up poorer than some of the black kids getting into universities on Affirmative Action. Why shouldn't I get that leg up instead?" The thing is, one can never just judge racism on an individual level alone. It's also historic and systemic—remember, white people will never not have that several-century head start.

Believe me, I sympathize with feeling like the work you put in isn't paying off, like you deserve something you didn't get, like odds are stacked against you. That said, there's a big difference between a kind of unfairness that happens to you as the result of a sincere and clear policy that is trying to right decades of wrongdoing and the kind of unfairness that is pursued as an end itself—like Jim Crow laws that lasted from 1870 to 1965. Think about that: The unfairness black people have experienced has been the point of systemic racism, not the result of some other, more noble effort. What white people experience as unfairness as a result of Affirmative Action does not have as its aim being unfair to white people. And therein lies the main difference.

Another white-talk argument concerns the twenty-eight days of February, otherwise known as Black History Month. When I was in middle school, the first day of every February's Black History Month was signified by fried chicken and corn bread being served in the cafeteria. I guess it was to fit the stereotype that black people love fried chicken. Thinking back, that was pretty racially insensitive, but I won't complain—the chicken was good! But during these cafeteria conversations with my friends, it was often asked, "Why can't white people have White History Month?" Let me take this from the top. Black History Month exists because of a black scholar named Dr. Carter G. Woodson, who in 1915 founded the Association for the Study of Negro Life and History (ASNLH). To promote awareness of black achievements, Dr. Woodson and his colleagues created Negro History and Literature Week, soon renamed Negro Achievement Week. They marked the week in February because it was the birth month of both Frederick Douglass and Abraham Lincoln, men who played an integral role in shaping black history. Negro Achievement Week caught on like a stadium cheer: By the 1950s, it had expanded into a monthlong celebration, and in 1976, that shift was made official with the renaming of Negro

History Week into Black History Month. Every American president since the 1970s has endorsed that commemoration with an official proclamation.

Let me tell you why there's no White History Month. There's no White History Month because we celebrate the accomplishments of white people Every. Single. Day. White people have always been esteemed in this country, have always been celebrated. Black people have had to push to celebrate themselves and their culture in public. You ever read about the first black person to do so and so, or hold such and such a job? I know I have. Here's the first black head football coach in the NFL. Here's the first black owner in the NFL. Here's the first black editor in chief of *Harper's Bazaar*. Here's the first black person to attend Harvard, the first black valedictorian at Princeton. Here's the first black woman to win a Pulitzer Prize. Now think of when you've ever heard about the first white person to do something significant. I can't remember ever reading, "Check it out, finally a white person's done this!" And you know why? Because white people have had a lock on significance since before this country was even a country. They've had a lock on opportunities, and they've had a lock on the institutions that report achievements, too. White people are celebrated every day for the things they do. It's simply called the news. It's called the history books. It's called Mount Rushmore. It's called the White House. They're called Fortune 500 CEOs and college presidents and venture capitalists and Oscar winners.

All to say: No, it's not reverse racism to celebrate Black History Month. But it's probably racist to call for a White History Month.

For similar reasons, it's insensitive to say, "All lives matter," when someone says, "Black Lives Matter." White lives have never been in danger from black lives to the degree that black lives have been endangered by white people and whiteness—and that's on an individual level and a systemic level. Some people say "All lives matter" to provoke conflict and others might do it for the sake of inclusivity. Still, in either instance, it's insensitive and harmful. Novelist Jason Reynolds does a wonderful job of expanding on the reasons why:

> If you say, "No, all lives matter," what I would say is I believe that you believe all lives matter. But because I live the life that I live, I am certain that in this country, all lives [don't] matter. I know for a fact that, based on the numbers, my life hasn't mattered; that black women's lives definitely haven't mattered, that black trans people's lives haven't mattered, that black gay people's lives haven't mattered . . . that immigrants' lives don't matter, that Muslims' lives don't matter. The Indigenous people of this country's lives have never mattered. I mean, we could go on and on and on. So, when we say "all lives," are we talking about White lives? And if so, then let's just say that. 'Cause it's coded language.

Think about it this way, friends. If your neighbor is sick with bone cancer and holds a rally on their front lawn to raise money for bone cancer research, would it be appropriate for someone to show up at the rally and yell, "Stop talking about bone cancer. All cancers matter!"? No, of course it wouldn't be. Do I agree that people suffering with all types of cancers matter? Yes, most definitely. But when someone or some group is addressing their specific pain or condition, it's important to listen to their story and sympathize with them, not to try to shift the topic or language to something that makes *you* feel more comfortable. So when black people proclaim black lives matter, they are not saying white lives don't matter. It is a given in this country that they do. We're taught that from the moment we pick up our first picture book. What people are really and truly saying is that black lives matter as well as white lives. Add to that list of false equivalents: black pride versus white pride, white privilege versus "black privilege." That last phrase is about as real as reverse racism.

LET'S GET UNCOMFORTABLE

I consider myself a pretty sensible guy. And for me, a "fair" argument is one where there's probably some merit on both sides, where any reasonable, thoughtful person is looking for a path to compromise. So I get that somewhere there's a person used to hearing out arguments that say, "Well, if white people can be racist against black people, surely there must be *some* merit on the other side?" And here's my answer: Don't fall for it! This simply isn't that kind of conversation. Remember words have meanings, and *white* and *black* just aren't equal in this country, for all the systemic reasons we've mentioned. They can't be easily switched around because of what those labels have meant historically.

Still, it's an uncomfortable conversation for a lot of reasons. For one, it makes all white people accountable.

And I know that's hard to think you're paying for the wrongs of someone else. It's also hard because who doesn't want to be proud of what they've done, to be proud of what their ancestors have done? I feel you on that. Really, I do. But if you are going to be proud of the history of white people, you have to acknowledge the *whole* history of white people. And if we put all those great things in context, we must admit that they occurred in an America that rigged, that denied opportunities to others, so that white people could thrive. And this is not to dismiss the talent, intelligence, drive, ingenuity of all the great white people. Not to dismiss all those firsts from long ago and even now. But if we're going to talk about it, let's talk about all of it.

TALK IT, WALK IT

It will take courage, empathy, and commitment to challenge those who rely on white talk. If your goal is to fight racism, to help foster an America that isn't built on white privilege, then you'll have to do your part. Each and every one of you will have to do your part. Educate white friends and family on Black History Month. Talk to them about why calling for a White History Month not only isn't needed but is actually another act of racism. Discuss with them how racism is on the hands of white people in general as well as white people in particular, how even though they might not believe themselves overtly racist, that they could be acting in a way that fosters racism or fails to discourage it.

To get more information about racism, a good place to start is at your local or school library. Reach out to your teacher or librarian for a few books on the topic. One book you can ask for is *This Book Is Anti-Racist: 20 Lessons on How to Wake Up, Take Action, and Do the Work* by Tiffany Jewell. If you can make it to D.C., I encourage you to visit the wonderful National Museum of African American History and Culture, or if you can't, there may be a black (it's likely called

African American) museum closer to you. If you're really excited about education, I suggest checking out these documentaries on race, racism, and black studies on the internet:

- How America Invented Race | The History of White People in America
  (youtube.com/watch?v=ppvbBY3ce8Y)
- The Talk—Race in America
  (video.kpbs.org/video/talk-race-america-talk
  -race-america/)
- The African Americans—Many Rivers to Cross
  (video.kpbs.org/show/african-americans-many
  -rivers-cross/)

While you're out there living your life every day, pay attention to how many times you hear something being touted as the first black X. And how long it took for that thing to happen. Think about how weird it would sound to hear of the first white X to do something. If you're in a room with a bunch of powerful people, take note of how many of them are white. Ask yourself: Would it have felt unusual if most of them were black? As you go throughout your days, pay attention to how often white is the default—remember the thought exercise we did at the beginning of this chapter? Know that saying "all lives matter" means arguing that we're still not defaulting to white enough.

"*Why can't We (the rules/ government) just start over?*"

THE FIX

Who's Governing the Government

> I'm not a Republican, nor a Democrat, nor an
> American, and got sense enough to know it.
> I'm one of the 22 million black victims of the
> Democrats, one of the 22 million black victims of
> the Republicans, and one of the 22 million black
> victims of Americanism. And when I speak, I
> don't speak as a Democrat, or a Republican, (nor
> an American) I speak as a victim of America's
> so-called democracy. You and I have never seen
> democracy; all we've seen is hypocrisy.
>
> **—MALCOLM X,**
> **"The Ballot or the Bullet"** *(1964)*

Young peoples, let me remind you that I was born
and raised in Dallas, Texas. During the 2016 election,

when Donald Trump faced off against Hillary Clinton for the presidency, I was living it up in my hometown—in a very nice part of the city, I might add—and looking for a polling station, the place you go to cast your vote. Wouldn't you know it, there was one at this church right by my house. This was my first time voting in Texas. (I had been in Cleveland for the last election, playing football for the Browns.) That is to say, I didn't know what to expect and was thinking that the polling station might have a crazy line. But when I pulled up to the church, there was nobody there except six or seven poll workers. I waltzed right inside, said hi to the nice white staffers, filled out my little ballot, submitted it, and waltzed my smiling self right back out. The whole thing took maybe three and a half minutes, hellos and goodbyes included.

Now compare that to the 2018 midterm election, when America had the opportunity to vote for their congressional representatives—the folks who speak for your state in Congress. At that time, I was living in

Austin, Texas. My house was in a gentrifying area—code for "not so nice part of town where white folks are moving in"—on the east side of town that was still made up of mostly working-class black people. My closest polling station ended up being a Fiesta grocery store. To vote that year, I pulled up to Fiesta with the confidence of a dude who'd last voted in an affluent neighborhood, thinking I was going to walk my happy little butt into another polling station and zippity-do-dah right out. But when I turned the corner to park, I saw a line of at least two hundred people. *Man*, I thought, *what is this?* I walked inside to investigate and saw the line snaking around the store and back outside. I couldn't believe it. "Is this the line to vote," I asked, "or are they giving out free trips to the Bahamas?" They were like, "No, no, no, this is the line to vote."

I was tempted to leave. I had a flight to catch; I didn't have two and a half hours to wait in line. But there was this sweet old black woman in front of me, and she said, "You'd better stay here, son. Remember all we went through to vote." I looked at her. I waited in that line.

Why do I bring up these two examples of voting? I want you to see how some Americans have better privilege than others when it comes to voting. The first example, when I went to the church in the wealthier, whiter neighborhood, illustrates how people with money in America, mostly white people, have easier access to voting for their elected officials. The second example, when I had to go to the grocery store in the working-class side of town and stand in line for over two hours with two hundred other people just to vote, shows you how other Americans have their access to voting limited because of poor access to the ballot box.

Now picture this. While I was breezing through a polling station in 2016, not far away in Fort Worth, Texas, a woman named Crystal Mason walked to her local station to do what that old woman in Austin had reminded me to stay for. Mason, a mother of three, might not have voted had her mother not convinced her that it would set a good example for her kids. Mason trooped down to her local polling station, and to her surprise, her name wasn't registered on the voting rolls. Determined, she cast a provisional ballot, meant to be approved pending further checks. Mason was formerly in prison and as it turns out missed the fine print on her ballot that read, "I understand that it is a felony of the second degree to vote in an election for which I know I am not eligible." Not only did Mason fail to see the words, she was also unaware of Texas's super strict voting laws, the ones that actually made her ineligible to vote.

Three months after she voted, she was called into a Fort Worth courthouse, handcuffed, and charged with voter fraud. A year or so later, she was convicted of fraud and sentenced to the harshest penalty possible: five years in prison. It hardly seemed a fair judgment for the small oversight of a woman and mother of three who believed she was doing her civic duty.

Is America really a democracy? The short answer is no, it's technically a republic, or what some people term a *representative democracy*. Our laws are made by representatives we have chosen (in theory), who must comply with a constitution that is built (in theory) to protect the rights of the minority from the will of the majority. But the truest answer is that America has never been a republic for everyone who lives within its borders.

So we've got systemic racism, right? All these institutions like housing, schools, and prisons, that keep disadvantaging people of color. You may have been asking yourself: If we have laws keeping these systems in place, why not just make new laws? Why not vote out racist people and practices? This chapter is about why not. There are tools, it turns out, by which (some of) those in power are still actively perpetuating racist systems and disenfranchising those who would change things—a.k.a. the voters. I call this whole situation the Fix. If we want an America that's not fundamentally racist, we must address the Fix, like, yesterday.

LET'S REWIND

Two of the most rigged parts of our democratic system are voting and jury duty. If you've never heard of jury duty, think of it as the service that people, called *jurors*, do by listening to court cases and deciding if the accused person is guilty or innocent of the crimes they are charged with. It's kind of like those murder mystery games you play with your friends where you have to decide who the bad guy is, except it's not a game. Both of these services—voting and jury duty—are civic duties that American citizens share. Each has been corrupted with more discrimination than we could cover in all four quarters and overtime of a tight football game, so in the interest of space, I'll focus on the long history of voter suppression of black people and the destructive practice of rigging juries against black folks (and other POC).

You might've learned about a little thing called the electoral college. Yes, the confounding institution that awarded the 2016 election to Donald Trump and the 2000 election to George W. Bush, despite their opponents winning the popular vote in each case. In 2000, Bush won 271 electoral votes but lost the popular vote by about 500,000 ballots. Years later, in 2016, Donald Trump won the electoral college majority with 304 votes while losing the popular vote by 2.9 million ballots. But each man still became president. Wonder why? You might remember, class, that the electoral college was created because, during the Constitutional Convention in 1787, it's commonly taught that the Founding Fathers thought ordinary Americans wouldn't have enough information to make informed and intelligent voting decisions. While that may have been true, there was also another major factor, what I call the *electoral fix*, being hashed out between Northern and Southern delegates. This "fix" revolved around the question of what to do about 500,000 or so enslaved people living in the country at the time. How should they be counted? The result of that debate was what became known as the Three-Fifths Compromise.

Article 1, section 2 of the Constitution, states: "Representatives and direct taxes shall be apportioned among the several states which may be included within this Union, according to their respective numbers, which shall be determined by adding to the whole number of free persons, including those bound to service for a term of years, and excluding Indians not taxed, three fifths of all other persons." In other words, the compromise counted each enslaved person as three fifths of a human being for the purposes of taxes and representation. That agreement gave the Southern states more electoral votes than if they hadn't been counted at all, but fewer votes than if black people had been counted as a full person. That political leverage paved the way for nine of the first twelve presidents being slave-owning Southerners.

Keep in mind, those enslaved black people couldn't vote themselves, couldn't own property, nor take advantage of any of the other privileges available to white men. Not only was all their labor stolen from them, their bodies were symbolically used to grant their enslavers more power. If we're talking an electoral fix, the Three-Fifths Compromise is the ultimate.

A century later, on December 6, 1865, the Thirteenth Amendment abolished slavery, thus gutting the Three-Fifths Compromise. The Fourteenth Amendment then granted formerly enslaved people citizenship and gave black people supposed "equal protection under the law," while the Fifteenth Amendment declared, "The right of citizens of the United States to vote shall not be denied or abridged by the United States or by any State on account of race, color, or previous condition of servitude." That's a lot of fancy lingo to say now that black men are citizens, they can vote, and no government can try to stop them from doing it.

Between 1863 and 1877, newly freed black Americans tasted democracy for the first time. They started their own towns, voted in elections, and many black men even held elective offices throughout the South and in the federal government. In a sense, the goal of this Reconstruction period was for the South to rebuild itself to look more like the racial social order of the North—general equality of all races in regard to work and voting rights in the eyes of the law (at least on paper—we all know the North had its own flavor of racism). This "reconstruction" in the South was possible because the U.S. government kept Union soldiers from the North in the South to make sure black people could exercise their freedom. So game over? Of course not.

A little over ten years after the war, the Union Army—and by extension, the Northern states—pulled out of the South for the purpose of "healing the union." By doing so, they let the South have their way and thereby wasted all the promise of Reconstruction. The way I see it, those Northern states were the original devil's bargainers: the fixers who, to ensure their own power, agreed that freedom didn't have to mean power for black people. They left black people without protection, and without that protection, without the enforcement of fairness and justice, racist white people figured out new ways to oppress them. It wasn't long before Southern states were inventing ways to skirt the Fourteenth and Fifteenth Amendments and keep black men and, later, black women (American women, of any race, could not legally vote until 1920, when the Nineteenth Amendment was passed) from participating in American democracy.

No better place to start than with what were called *grandfather clauses*. Beginning with Louisiana, seven states between the 1890s and early 1900s passed laws that allowed any person who'd been granted the right to vote before 1867 to continue voting without special requirements. It was called a *grandfather clause* because white men (remember, women were decades away from winning the right to vote) were literally *grandfathered in.* Since most black people had been enslaved prior to 1867, they were denied the opportunity to vote based on the clauses. They still had to be allowed to vote, legally, but states kept their black citizens from voting by requiring poll taxes (it's exactly what you think: paying a fee to enter the voting polls), literacy tests (remember, reading and writing had been forbidden for black people during slavery), property ownership, and even constitutional quizzes (how does one pass one such test when he can't read or has never even had access to the Constitution?).

The Northern states weren't angels, by the way. States like Massachusetts and Connecticut also passed grandfather clauses to limit the political power of black people and immigrants arriving from Europe.

Voter suppression laws are not just in the history books. They are in place right now, using new and improved tactics with the same old objective: to disenfranchise, or oppress, black people. Like in 2020 in Kansas where a Republican secretary of state, Kris Kobach, championed a law that required proof of citizenship to vote on the grounds that non-citizens were voting illegally. That law was struck down because the U.S. Circuit Court of Appeals said that Kobach, a white man, "failed to prove the additional burden on voters [to prove their citizenship] was justified by actual evidence of fraud." During the time the law was in effect, thirty-one thousand potential voters were prevented from voting, yet the federal appeals court noted that no more than thirty-nine non-citizens had managed to vote in the past nineteen years. Other states, including Arkansas, Pennsylvania, and North Carolina, have enacted similar voter ID laws, citing claims of voters using "fraudulent" IDs. This despite these ACLU stats: Up to 25 percent of black citizens of voting age lack government-issued ID, compared to only 8 percent of white people. Why do one out of four black people lack a government-issued identification? There are many reasons. Most people use their license as their government-issued ID, but not everyone knows how to drive or has had the opportunity to own a car. Others might use their passport, but passports cost money (and time) to obtain. And if you have no plans to travel outside of the country, it may seem like an unnecessary cost. Another option is a state-issued ID, but if a person is down on their luck or homeless, they may not be able to afford one.

Other strategies of voter suppression, a.k.a. the Fix, are state lawmakers increasing or decreasing the number of polling stations in a given district, changing the times or days the stations are open, and even planting faulty machines in certain polling stations to slow them down. Another common tactic has been purging the registries of people who can vote. This is done by removing people from the voting registry who haven't voted for a certain number of years or haven't received a voting card mailed to their address. This more often targets black people and poor people who have unstable housing.

And then there's gerrymandering. This is when

a state redraws the boundary of a voting district so as to negate certain votes. Two ways to do this: One is "packing," where the boundaries are drawn in such a way that several voters for a particular party are clustered into a district already predicted to be a win, rendering a significant number of votes for that party useless because they would've won anyhow. The other is "cracking," which is when voting districts are drawn in such a way that voters for a party are broken into multiple districts, diluting their voting power and allowing the opposing candidate to win with a large majority. Both Democrats and Republicans use gerrymandering schemes, though the latter does so much more often.

There is one more election fix that's been getting attention in recent years: preventing people who've been convicted of a crime from voting. The length and kinds of restriction vary from state to state—from a lifetime ban up to people being disallowed to vote while incarcerated—and include restricting their ability to vote until they've completed parole, been released from jail on a temporary basis, or have paid certain fees. Barring currently or formerly incarcerated people from voting doesn't only suppress black voters, it targets them disproportionately, since they are overrepresented in prisons and jails. It also serves the double objective of weakening the Democratic popular vote, since black voters are more likely to vote on the side of liberal Democrats.

Sometimes these tactics fail, luckily. In 2020, the Wisconsin legislature, headed by Republicans, tried to protect a conservative Wisconsin Supreme Court position using clever tactics to restrict voter turnout for the Democratic Party. At the height of the coronavirus pandemic, they attempted to curtail mail-in voting (invaluable for Democratic voters living near crowded inner-city polling stations and who have inflexible work schedules) by insisting on in-person voting. Their plan backfired, however, and instead inspired a huge voter turnout that helped to unseat the conservative majority. In the same year, a Florida federal judge ruled that a state law requiring felons to pay any outstanding fines before registering to vote is unconstitutional.

Too often, though, voter suppression succeeds.

Would it surprise you that another part of the Fix involves our courts and, in particular, our juries? Bryan Stevenson, a lawyer and activist who's dedicated his life to social justice, describes American courts this way: "We have a system of justice that treats you better if you're rich and guilty than if you're poor and innocent." I would add to his adjective of *poor* the adjective of *black*.

Maybe no person knows this better than Timothy Foster, a black man who in 1987 was convicted by an all-white jury in Georgia of murdering a white woman and sentenced to life in prison. As Americans, one of our constitutional rights, if we go to trial for a criminal offense, is that we get to have a jury of our peers. They are the ones who hear the case and then decide if we are guilty or not. This is supposed to be a way to reduce the chances of bias in the jury.

But Foster didn't get a jury of his peers. His case ended up before the U.S. Supreme Court, where it was discovered that Georgia prosecutors had stricken black people from his pool of possible jurors, using a process known as *peremptory strikes*. The Supreme Court had ruled the selection of jurors by race to be unconstitutional just a year before Foster's trial, so prosecutors could no longer legally, intentionally appoint an all-white jury to judge his case. So they created a loophole called *peremptory strikes*: a playbook of "race-neutral" reasons to strike a black juror from a case. News flash: One of those unjust reasons is often found valid.

A little recap here. For almost a century, black people were not allowed to legally vote, even as their bodies (three fifths each) were used to beef up the Southern vote. Then they got the legal right to vote, only to face all kinds of despicable tactics to keep them from it. This practice of using literacy tests, intimidation, and poll taxes to keep black people from the ballot box didn't end until 1970. Five years after the passing of the Voting Rights Act and a hundred years after black men were granted the right to vote under the Fifteenth Amendment. They then face a justice system not of their peers but of white people (as of 2017, 71 percent of U.S. district court judges were white), who, due to the biases mentioned earlier in this chapter, send them to prison far more often than white people. Once freed, they face yet more obstacles when trying to vote. Like Crystal Mason, should they somehow vote by accident, they face more prison. Should they not vote, well, they have little means of changing unfair laws and those who make them.

A lose-lose situation, whichever way you look at it. That, young brothers and sisters, is the nature of the Fix.

LET'S GET UNCOMFORTABLE

Because of voter suppression, there are fewer polling stations in places of lower socioeconomic status, particularly liberal (majority Democratic) cities in Republican states. Back when I was in Dallas, my fancy neighborhood with the breezy voting experience was also a Republican area. But in Austin, I lived in a gentrifying area with a historically lower socioeconomic status. What I remember from that day in 2018 was that several people left the line, and if I had to guess, I'd say some of them left because they couldn't afford to take more time off from work.

Our democracy is supposed to be fair and impartial, but the truth is that both Republicans and Democrats engage in the Fix to some degree (though it must be said, Republicans are far guiltier). You don't need to be a political scientist to see how unfair the political system has been to black people. We must continue to bring up these tough conversations, between each other, on our social media platforms, in our newspapers, and so on.

Crystal Mason waived her right to a jury. You have to wonder, why would a black woman in Texas waive her right to be tried by a jury of her peers? You have to wonder if it was because Mason did not believe she would get a fair trial by jury. You might wonder whether Sharon Wilson, the Republican district attorney who aggressively pursued the case, would have used peremptory strikes to ensure just that. In any case, I doubt that a fair jury, one that included black people and POC, would have decided to send a mother to prison for mistakenly filling out a provisional ballot. Instead of a jury, Mason's fate was solely in the hands of District Judge Ruben Gonzalez, who decided that Mason should do five years of prison time for overlooking some fine print.

"It doesn't make any sense," Mason said in an interview with *The Guardian*. "Why would I vote if I knew I was not eligible? What's my intent? What was

I to gain by losing my kids, losing my mom, potentially losing my house? I have so much to lose, all for casting a vote." She appealed her sentence and was denied. Now, I get it. Mason's intent was not to break the law, but her actions did so anyway. That's why we have juries—because laws are imperfect, and part of a jury's job is to find gray areas that the law misses. To close the gap between the law and the people it's meant to serve.

Meanwhile, in the very same county where Mason voted that year, a judge named Russ Casey pleaded guilty to turning in fake signatures to secure a place on a Texas primary ballot. His crime was not, in any way, an accident or oversight. It was a premeditated affront to our political system. Casey pleaded guilty to committing that crime, and for his guilty plea, the Texas courts sentenced him to two years in jail—then changed his two-year prison sentence to a five-year sentence of probation, where instead of jail time, he was free to live his life as long as he played by the rules set by his probation officer. Can you believe that? A five-year sentence upheld on appeal for a black woman versus a two-year sentence commuted into probation for a white man. The Fix was in way back when. And the Fix is in right this second. That's the bad news. But fear not, young brothers and sisters. The good news is that the law is not fixed, but fixable. It's a living thing, constantly changing and reforming. And together, we can make it better for everyone.

TALK IT, WALK IT

Young folks, you're not old enough to vote yet, but your grown-ups are. You can encourage them to use their vote by sharing this information with them. Go to usa.gov/absentee-voting to find out about mail-in voting in your state. You can find general information as well as a link to your state's local election office for specific rules in your state. You can also visit vote.org /polling-place-locator/ to find the polling stations in your state or community.

If you're in Texas, call your elected official and demand that Crystal Mason be released from jail. If you're elsewhere, visit the American Civil Liberties Union, which, among other things, launches legal battles against voter suppression all over the country. Their website (aclu.org/issues/voting-rights/fighting-voter-suppression) has a whole tab of resources on the subject. You can also encourage your parents or adults in your life to donate some money to the organization if their means allow it.

You can also encourage the grown-ups in your life or school to volunteer at a local community organization or shelter, a place where you can encounter citizens who might not be as informed on the voting process and their particular voting rights. You guys can also help register voters, especially in areas with a high number of black people and/or POC and/or poor people. As with systemic racism, the issues are countless, but so are the ways to help.

One more note: Remind the adults in your life not

to forget about local elections. State legislatures have a huge influence on what you can and can't do where you live; the mayor approves the city budget on things like police or school funding; your local district attorney has say over who goes to prison and who doesn't. Local elections can even get your potholes filled, and I think we're all anti-potholes. So remind your folks to do their research on the candidates just as they would for a president. Attend their speeches and debates when they can, call them out on issues of fairness and bias. And most of all, push them to vote, vote, vote, vote, like their and your lives depend on it. Like all of our lives depend on it. Because they do.

*"Why do some people hate
black people? Or why would
someone want to hurt them?"*

THUG LIFE

Justice for Some

They kill or maim on impulse, without any
intelligible motive ... The buzz of impulsive
violence, the vacant stares and smiles, and the
remorseless eyes ... they quite literally have no
concept of the future ... they place zero value on
the lives of their victims, whom they reflexively
dehumanize ... capable of committing the most
heinous acts of physical violence for the most
trivial reasons ... for as long as their youthful
energies hold out, they will do what comes
"naturally": murder, rape, rob, assault, burglarize,
deal deadly drugs, and get high.

—CRIMINOLOGIST JOHN DILULIO,
coining the term superpredator *in the* Washington Examiner, *1995*

When I hear *gang member*, I think about how some people join gangs because they want to feel protected, to feel safe, or fit in. I think of people like Michael, Jessica, and Damien. Michael, known to his friends as Puppet, joined a gang when he was thirteen years old. As part of his initiation, Michael was beaten up by the other gang members. "You got to take a beatdown by your homies just to show them you're tough," he said. He decided to join the gang because that's what all his neighborhood friends were doing. He didn't really know his dad, and his mother worked a lot, so the gang became his family.

When Jessica joined a gang in Chicago, she was just a kid looking to make fast money and for someone to love her. She didn't have a good relationship with her mother or any other adults in her life. "I joined a gang to be loved," Jessica said, "and I had to find out the hard way that the streets don't love you."

Damien, known to his friends as Pacman, first got involved with a gang when he was just nine years old.

He joined as a means of survival. "I had nothing to do, I had no guidance," he said. "So I was raised to be knocked on the streets, running around, looking at the older guys, what they had that I didn't have, and I wanted that."

Now you're probably thinking, *These stories are sad, but why is Acho telling us this?* Take another look at the quote that opened this chapter. Now think about why each of the young people mentioned above joined a gang in the first place. Do they sound like the mindless, bloodthirsty predators the quote described? No, they don't. But they are the types of young people the quote was designed to turn into villains. To make millions of Americans afraid of.

Each of them—Michael, Jessica, and Damien—were just kids looking for things that would come from being raised in a healthy, stable home. Something that none of them had growing up. Without the supportive family they needed, they each found their way into a gang that promised to give them what they were missing: love, safety, and a sense of belonging.

Why is this important to note? Keep reading, my friends.

Let's visit a scene from 1995, where someone decided to hate a group of people on the strength of inherited prejudice. It happened at the White House, when a Princeton professor and criminologist named John Dilulio was invited to attend a working dinner with President Clinton on juvenile crime. At that dinner, Dilulio introduced Clinton to a term he'd invented: the *superpredator*. See the top of the chapter for his, uh, colorful definition.

As you might imagine, Dilulio's description had a lot of people scared. And while he didn't say all super-predators were black, at that dinner and again later, he did point out that trouble would be greatest in inner-city *black* neighborhoods. He also took care to remind people that their violence would spill into the suburbs (the last thing white suburbanites wanted to hear). That was bad enough, but maybe the most damaging theory Dilulio presented was that the kids were doing what came "naturally" to them, as if violence was coded in their DNA, as if there was an entire generation of young black sociopaths. Remember the Angry Black Man, my friends?

Fear, young brothers and sisters, is a powerful emotion. It can drive people to do hurtful things. Couple that fear with centuries-old stereotypes and you've got your answer as to why white people felt justified in labeling a whole generation of black youth as superpredators.

Ugly as it was, the idea of the superpredator caught on. It had a champion in Hillary Clinton, who talked it up in a stump speech for her husband's anti-crime agenda. His goal, she said, was "to take back our streets from crime, gangs, and drugs . . . We need to take these people on . . . They are not just gangs of kids anymore. They are often the kinds of kids that are called superpredators. No conscience. No empathy. We can talk about why they ended up that way, but first we have to bring them to heel."

Let's stop for a moment and take this in. By Hillary Clinton's way of thinking, kids who joined gangs weren't hurting young people looking for help and belonging in the wrong place—remember Michael, Jessica, and Damien?—but were instead immoral, stone-cold criminals who needed to be locked up before they killed somebody.

That same thinking birthed President Clinton's now notorious 1994 crime bill, technically called the Violent Crime Control and Law Enforcement Act. This implemented things like a "three strikes" mandatory life sentence for repeat offenders, provided funding for hiring one hundred thousand new police officers, and also provided a whopping $9.7 billion for new prisons. It also expanded the kinds of offenses that could earn a death penalty. The bill, coupled with the image of the superpredator, helped create the conditions of mass incarceration we see today.

Young brothers and sisters, this chapter's another bumpy ride. The tricky thing with crime and punishment in the black community is that there is a lot of real, tragic violence being committed, often against other black people—and it's too often dismissed as "black-on-black crime," somehow less worthy of notice than the ever-feared "black-on-white" crime. This violence is, in itself, the product of the systemic racism in ways we've already talked a bit about. At the same time, the policing and incarceration of black bodies is rampant and unjust, made worse in no small part by the racist specters of the superpredator, the gangbanger, the thug. It's time to untangle the reality from the fiction.

LET'S REWIND

The way people talk about black violence and street gangs, you'd think we invented the whole shebang. Yes, the Crips and Bloods and Latin Kings are infamous for a reason, but the first gangs in America were actually white people, formed shortly after the Revolutionary War (one of their less celebrated firsts). After early American immigration picked up in the 1800s, on-their-way-to-white gangs emerged. One of the earliest gangs in America, the Irish American Five Points Gang, is still recognized by some experts as the most significant gang in American history. And yet, somehow, white men as a whole have not been marred by the Five Points Gang's history of violence.

Black and Latinx folks didn't get into the gang scene at all until the early twentieth century and didn't really get cooking until the 1950s and '60s. The Crips and the Bloods are black gangs, both formed in poverty-stricken South Central Los Angeles, California. The Crips were formed in the late 1960s by guys named Raymond Washington and Tookie Williams and were originally styled after the Black Panther Party—a black militant group fighting for civil rights. The Crips ruled the day for a few years until a rival gang named the Bloods was formed in Compton by high schoolers Sylvester Scott and Benson Owens. Back then, their role was to provide protection from other neighborhood gangs, as well as to combat police harassment. However, by the early 1980s, the rival gang violence escalated so far that hundreds of gang-related murders were happening within the black community every year. I give you that history to say that gangs are brutal, organized criminal enterprises. But, peoples, there is so much in black communities, even among young men with gang ties, that goes beyond that. Yet all black communities suffer the consequences of gang stereotypes.

Though it might seem ironic, the term *black-on-black crime* was started by black people in the 1970s, particularly by people writing about crime in Chicago, Illinois. Soon after the phrase was coined, black civil rights leader Jesse Jackson (the guy who had run for president and campaigned for the term African American) started to chastise white government officials and media for "their silence and ineffectiveness in dealing with the present black-on-black crime crisis." Jackson was calling out the unfairness of the criminal justice system, where black people convicted of crimes against white people received harsher sentences than they did for crimes committed against black people in their own communities. This meant that black victims of violence were less likely to see justice.

By the 1980s, the term had been thrown around enough for it to stick in the public consciousness. But it had also been transformed from a well-intentioned critique of a neglectful and biased justice system into a weapon for white people to argue that violence is inherent to black communities, and for them to begin drafting policies that made the problem worse. Truth be told, black communities are over-policed *and* under-policed. By that, I mean, when policing happens, it is not to investigate real crimes or to deter criminal activity. Too often, what passes as policing is the never-ending harassment of black residents for petty or trumped-up offenses, while serious crimes go unsolved. The more this dynamic happens, the less black people trust the cops, and the less effective police officers are in serving the neighborhood. It's a sad but true reality in black communities throughout America.

These days, many opponents of the Black Lives Matter movement often trot out the statistic that the majority of black people are killed by black people, and ask why us black folks care about white-on-black crime—specifically, death by police officer—more than black-on-black crime. We don't. Black people care about being murdered, period. In addition to its murky origins, *black-on-black crime* is a misleading term without context. The most important bit of context: people generally commit crimes against people of the same race. The majority of violent crimes against white people are perpetrated by white people. But I've never heard anyone in my life (have you?)

reference white people killing white people as "white-on-white crime."

You want to know the truth? Poverty, not race, is a more accurate predictor of who commits crimes. Black-on-black crime exists, but it's the product of, among other systemic factors I've discussed, segregated housing, concentrated poverty, and unequal schooling. According to the Bureau for Justice Statistics, people living in households with income below the federal poverty line are twice as likely to commit violent crime than people living in high-income households, regardless of race. We've been doing it wrong. The best tough-on-crime bill is a tough—the toughest—on-poverty bill.

Yes, we understand that there's an issue with crime in many black communities, and we certainly want to address it. But what we don't need and can't stand is the stigma that crime is only a black problem. Let me say this, too: Neither violent policing nor mass incarceration is the answer. You ever heard of the saying that numbers don't lie? Well, check out some of the statistics from the report *An Unjust Burden: The Disparate Treatment of Black Americans in the Criminal Justice System*:

- Black men make up about 13 percent of the U.S. male population but nearly 35 percent of all men who are under state or federal jurisdiction with a sentence of more than one year.
- One in 3 black men born in 2001 can expect to be incarcerated in his lifetime, compared to 1 in 6 Latino men and 1 in 17 white men.
- Black people are incarcerated in state prisons at a rate 5.1 times greater than that of white people.
- One in 18 black women born in 2001 will be incarcerated sometime in her life, compared to 1 in 45 Latina women and 1 in 111 white women.
- Forty-four percent of incarcerated women are black, although black women make up about 13 percent of the female U.S. population.

It's easy to say that black people, black men especially, are being over-policed. The above spells it out in hard data. And this isn't something out of the blue but the predictable outcomes of years of racist policies.

Now that we have this background, I want to get into something you may encounter on the regular. If you've heard anyone talk about gangs and violence, you may have heard them use the word *thug*. If you sift through your memory, I bet you can remember other instances of black people being called *thug*, have heard police or a politician use *thug* to describe a black man in the inner city, an aggressive protestor, or someone who steps out of the bounds of what white people deem normal.

It actually comes from the Hindi word *thuggee*, which means "deceiver" or "thief" or "swindler." Thugs stole and murdered in India for over five hundred years. The word didn't catch on in America until Mark Twain wrote about them in the 1800s, in work that colored the word with the connotation of a gangster. Back then, white people had American thugism on straight lock. (Remember, black people were still enslaved, or in other words, didn't possess the freedom to even be thugs.) But since *thug* always had a negative connotation, and since white people have been crafting negative stereotypes about black people from the jump, it was easy to paint them as thugs after the Civil War and for it to catch on.

Now I'm not going to sit here and say that the term doesn't fit the behavior of some people, black people included, but I also want you to remember something when you hear people using it. Calling someone a thug is putting them on a continuum that ends with a superpredator. It's a way of saying: This is what you *are*, not just what you do—or more often, what other people who look like you have done. A thug is the fictional archetype of Dilulio's nightmares, a stand-in for a black man that is hopelessly lost to violence, drugs, whatever; a vector of crime that needs to be feared and stopped, a caricature instead of a human being. And that kind of thinking is not what we need to fix either gang violence *or* over-policing in this country.

The bottom line: Our criminal justice system too often treats black people like thugs instead of like (white) people. So the cycle perpetuates, and both stereotypes and actual violence keep going and going and going.

LET'S GET UNCOMFORTABLE

First, a P.S. on *thug*. Just like with the N-word, black people do our best to take some of the sting out of it. You know the old saying, "If you can't run from it, run into it"? It's like that.

These days, there's Slim Thug and Young Thug, and I'm sure some other Thug-named rappers I don't know about. Go ahead and listen to them, go ahead and tell people Slim Thug's your fave. Just don't go calling people thugs.

And what about the fear of crime? Trust me, I get it. No one wants to knowingly put themselves in danger. But hurting innocent black people on the basis of stereotypes is not the answer. (White) America is steeped in stereotypes about the danger of black men, and when those mingle with the real statistics of disproportionate black arrests and incarceration, it can be hard to know what to believe when you're debating whether to cross the street in front of the guy in the hoodie. But you also have to consider many of the things I've been talking about in this book. We can't have the stereotype of black men as inherently dangerous without President Woodrow Wilson thinking *The Birth of a Nation* was "like writing history with lightning" in 1915, without all the lies and propaganda used to lynch black men, without black people being maligned as superpredators.

This book isn't going to make every reader suddenly lose all their biases. But for those who genuinely want to learn and evolve their thinking, I offer Hillary Clinton as an example. In 2016—at a fundraiser for her own presidential campaign—Clinton was confronted by a Black Lives Matter activist named

Ashley Williams. "I'm not a superpredator, Hillary Clinton. Can you apologize to black people for mass incarceration?" Williams said, while brandishing a sign that quoted Clinton's old words back to her: "We have to bring them to heel." Williams didn't get out much more than that before the audience started shushing her, and the Secret Service escorted her out of the building. Williams didn't get an answer from Clinton that day. But thank goodness for the viral cell phone videos. People saw the confrontation, and journalists started writing about it. And wouldn't you know it, in a *Washington Post* interview a few days later, Williams and black people across the country got their apology from Clinton: "In that speech, I was talking about the impact violent crime and vicious drug cartels were having on communities across the country and the particular danger they posed to children and families," said Clinton. "Looking back, I shouldn't have used those words, and I wouldn't use them today."

TALK IT, WALK IT

Next time you hear someone mention "black-on-black crime," educate them that it's a myth. You might start with a question: Do you know where the term *black-on-black crime* came from? Also, here's a language-born mindset change: Instead of saying *criminal justice reform*, just say *justice reform*. We get into sticky territory with the word *criminal*. Not that criminals don't exist, but that who gets called a criminal and why is not so cut-and-dried, and usually has something to do with race and class or both. Along those same lines, again, try to stop using the word *thug*, even as a joke. I hope I've made clear how harmful it can be. As the philosopher Norman Vincent Peale used to say, "Change your thoughts and change your world."

Read *Punching the Air* by Ibi Zoboi and Yusef Salaam. It's an important, powerful novel about young black men in the prison system. I also recommend *Dear Justyce* by Nic Stone. Two classic films that really get into the nuances of gangs and so-called thugs are John Singleton's *Boyz n the Hood* and the Hughes Brothers' *Menace II Society*. If you're really interested in understanding the plight of young black men in gangs, check out both of them. Also try the Ava DuVernay miniseries *When They See Us*, about the failure of justice known as the trial of the Central Park Five.

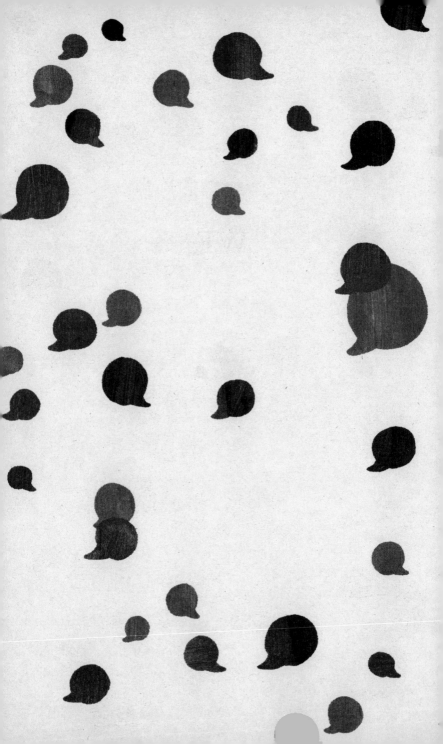

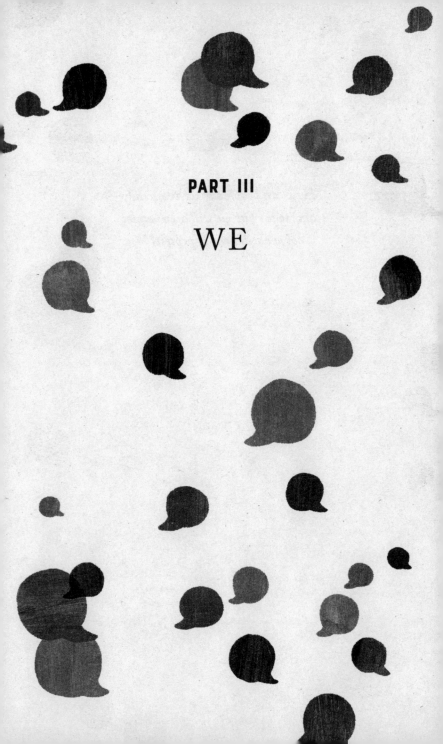

PART III

WE

"How can people say we've already
come so far but we still aren't equal
or we still need to protest?"

11

GOOD TROUBLE

Fighting for Change

The arc of the moral universe is long,
but it bends toward justice.

—DR. MARTIN LUTHER KING JR.,
March 31, 1968

We must come to see that human
progress never rolls in on the wheels
of inevitability. It comes through the
tireless efforts and the persistent work of
dedicated individuals who are willing to
be co-workers with God. And without
this hard work, time itself becomes an ally
of the primitive forces of social stagnation.
So we must help time and realize that the
time is always ripe to do right.

—DR. MARTIN LUTHER KING JR.,
March 31, 1968

During the protests in LA following the death of George Floyd, my friend told me a story. He said he was marching down Sunset Boulevard, past white people holding up their signs, past black people holding up their signs, past people holding hands and marching in unison, and almost everyone wearing their masks because of COVID. He looked to the right and saw a group of young black people.

"We're going down to Melrose and rob some people," one of them said. "We got to get them!"

My friend was like, "Uh, I got bad knees from playing football. And, uh, I had a couple MCL tears and a couple meniscus surgeries, so, um, I'm gonna have to take a pass, y'all." He let the black dudes go and kept on marching. A little later, he came upon some white people who were trying to take a photo and arguing about the best pose for Instagram.

"Here, hold the sign like this," one said.

"No, no, no, like this," the other said.

Did you catch that? Just like the black dudes that

wanted to strike back by robbing, the white people arguing over Instagram poses missed the whole point of the protest. Now, don't get me wrong. It's good to be excited about being part of something bigger than yourself like a protest movement. But both groups of people made it about themselves and their feelings. Maybe they didn't understand that the protest was about changing the way we do justice in America. My boy who watched both scenarios play out and does a lot of writing about peace and unity said that was it for him. He thought, *Man, let me just go home and write something. Everybody has a different way of protesting, and my pen is my sword.*

My friend's story reminds me of something that happened in my own family. Twelve-year-old me had just finished putting on my school uniform—gray slacks, white button-down, black shoes with white socks—when all of a sudden, I heard crying and screaming from downstairs. I ran down and saw my mother throwing herself into our living room wall. I mean this literally; she was hurling her own body at the wall, shoulder-first. It hurt to see. What was going on?

My dad told me that my mom's sister had died in Nigeria. I knew that my mom throwing herself into a wall wasn't going to bring her sister back, and I guessed she knew that, too. It would take me years to process what was really happening. It took me learning about the five stages of grief: denial, anger, bargaining, depression, and acceptance (FYI: not everyone goes through all the stages or experiences them in order). What I came to realize was that my mom was experiencing the anger stage of grief, and that she didn't know what to do with her anger, so she beat it against a wall.

Have you ever been angry and not known what to do with it? I know it's happened to me. I've learned our anger isn't always logical; heck, it's probably illogical most of the time. And because of that, it's something we often don't know how to express. So what about when this happens not to one person but a group? What about when this happens to a whole lot of black people? When you see people out protesting for George Floyd, or Ahmaud Arbery, or Emmett Till, or any of our beloved black people who have been murdered, what you're seeing is a group of angry people. About police violence, about systemic inequality, about the American dream that isn't yet real for everyone. Their protests take a lot of different forms, and even when they get violent—which I don't condone—what's really happening is just like my mother banging her shoulder against the wall.

The scenes of looting and destruction that so often light up the news and certain political rhetoric . . . they're only one end of the spectrum of black responses to the anger and frustration we've felt. An objectively small end, at that. The LA protests weren't defined by that group of dudes going down to Melrose any more than a stadium of one hundred thousand football fans is defined by the few who have a drunken brawl in the parking lot. So in this chapter, I'd like to consider the full range of my brothers' and sisters' cries against racism in this country, from MLK to BLM. We all know a change needs to come, and we're all figuring out how to fight for it.

I've had a million questions running through my own mind lately. Like, are protests necessary to effect change? Like, what are the most effective forms? Like, when does a protest become a riot, and who gets to decide? And is there some line when a riot against injustice becomes something else—a rebellion? Let's get into what I've learned.

LET'S REWIND

American protests date back to well before there was any such thing as the United States of America. You can't talk protest in these United States without mentioning those Sons of Liberty rebelling against taxation without representation by throwing all those chests of tea into Boston Harbor during the Revolutionary

War, or Nat Turner leading a rebellion of enslaved people in Virginia in 1831. The centuries since have seen a lot of ideas about what protests, justified and unjustified, look like.

As always, the words we use matter, and I want to focus on four of them here: *protest*, *riot*, *rebellion*, and *massacre*. When it comes to the fight against racism in this country, an ongoing question has been who gets to decide which is which, and then how they get to enforce those decisions. You may think the lines are pretty clear: A protest is generally understood as an orderly demonstration; a riot, not so much; a rebellion is an uprising; and a massacre is, well, a massacre—a tragedy of one-sided violence. And yet, as with so much else, it turns out that race has played a big part in how protests are viewed. And policed.

Unpacking these words a bit more, Henry David Thoreau coined the term *civil disobedience*—still the gold standard for non-violent protest everywhere. He described it as people prioritizing their conscience over the law but also expressing their grievances with civility. Or in plain speak, people's conscience inspiring them to protest, but with manners. *Civility* is the key word in Thoreau's definition. To help get an understanding of what's been considered civil over time, Thoreau refused to pay his taxes in protest of slavery, and Mahatma Gandhi went on hunger strikes, some of which lasted up to three weeks, in protest of the British occupation of India. There were the sit-ins that student leaders coordinated during the civil rights movement. These protests began in February of 1960, when four black students from North Carolina A&T College sat down at a Woolworth's lunch counter in Greensboro, North Carolina. Within two years, the protests spread to twenty states and included over seventy thousand black and white sit-in participants.

Civil disobedience is just one type of protest. There are many others. Imagine a long line that runs from left to right. This line is a scale. Milder and more positive forms of protests like boycotts, rallies, and civil disobedience sit to the left of our scale. Now, if we follow along that scale toward the right, eventually, we'll hit upon a less civil form of protest, rioting.

A *riot*, as defined by *Merriam-Webster*, is "a tumultuous disturbance of the public peace by three or more persons assembled together and acting with a common intent." One might even call it an *un*civil disturbance. Most people count looting and random violence to property as features of a riot.

A riot is also often defined by the race and class of people doing the rioting. The American version of riots have happened for all sorts of reasons—people agitating for labor unions, against Prohibition, over unemployment during the Depression ... but the race-related riots that took place before the mid-twentieth century were usually white mobs attacking black people. In Wilmington, North Carolina, in 1898, a two-thousand-strong mob of white supremacists, armed with rifles and pistols, staged the only coup d'état on American soil. They stormed into the city hall of Wilmington, overthrew the elected government, forced both black and white officials to resign, and ran many of them out of town. They stomped through black neighborhoods, shooting black people—many of them unarmed—and jailed others "for their own safety" before marching them to the train station and sending them out of town. They torched black newspapers. When it was all said and done, at least sixty black people were killed.

We've already seen another example of an American race riot: the tragedy in the Greenwood district of Tulsa, Oklahoma. The mob of white men that showed up at the county jail, intent on lynching one black man, was fifteen hundred strong; about seventy-five black men, many of them World War I veterans, showed up to protect him. Violence broke out when a white man tried to grab a black man's gun and it went off. Historians estimate that, when all was said and done, as many as 300 people had been killed.

Contrast this to the 1960s, when the nature of the conflicts shifted from white people attacking black people to black people resisting oppression. White people still called that resistance a *riot*, but black people described it as a *rebellion*—an often-armed resistance to an established government or ruler, in most cases to police and racist institutions. Or in other words, people rebelling against the power of an oppressive government. This is in contrast to the supposed spontaneity of a riot, which implies that there's no clear purpose or motive involved. A rebellion, on the other hand, implies that the actions are a response to injustice. Riot or rebellion. For rebellion, think Watts in 1965 (where violence sparked from an argument during a "routine" traffic stop of a black man resulted in the deaths of 34 people, thousands arrested, and millions of dollars in property damage over a seven-day span), or Detroit in 1967 (where police raided a black speakeasy and protests erupted that claimed the lives of 43 people, injured 342 others, and set fire to 1,400 buildings over the course of five days). Think of the small number of destructive and violent protests in places including Minnesota (more below) and LA during the Black Lives Matter movement.

Throughout all this history, white privilege has ruled how these conflicts were described. When it was white people instigating the violence, the media, politicians, law enforcement, and eventually historians minimized what was a literal massacre to a simple race riot. When black people started to initiate the protests, the media turned a rebellion into a riot—a description meant to portray all white people involved (citizens, property owners, businesspeople) as persecuted victims of unjustified black anger and hostility. They simultaneously made (white) policing of the situation, no matter how brutal, seem like a heroic or at least justified response.

A note on policing specifically. When race conflicts

have been instigated by white people, law enforcement has often responded on a wide spectrum, ranging from doing little to nothing, to encouraging other white people into participating or being participants themselves. When instigated by black people, they have strong-armed protestors, arrested them, killed them. *The Washington Post* reported that eight people were partially blinded by police tactics like tear gas during the first week of the 2020 Black Lives Matter protests that took place in numerous American cities. Remember, these were protests *against* police brutality. Over and over in the aftermath of black rebellion, law enforcement, predominantly white law enforcement, has invested in more "law and order"—a decision, you might guess, that tends to make things worse.

If you don't know, Black Lives Matter (BLM) began back in 2013 when black organizers Alicia Garza, Patrisse Cullors, and Opal Tometi created a black-centered political movement in response to a Florida jury acquitting George Zimmerman of murdering unarmed black seventeen-year-old Trayvon Martin. The movement really caught the nation's attention the following year during the protests in Ferguson, Missouri, over the fatal police shooting of unarmed black teenager Michael Brown. Since then, protests have been ignited all over the country, usually after the murder of a black person by a law enforcement officer—Tamir Rice in Cleveland, Eric Garner in New York, Alton Sterling in Baton Rouge.

What do you see when you look at the Black Lives Matter protests happening all around our world? And why do you see what you see?

One thing is for sure—there's still cause for Americans to feel aggrieved by their government. And at no time in recent history has this been more collectively acknowledged than during the protests spurred by the killings of George Floyd, Ahmaud Arbery, and Breonna Taylor, among others, in 2020. *The New York Times* estimated that fifteen to twenty-six million people demonstrated over George Floyd's death in the U.S. alone, making it the largest demonstration in the history of the country. Some researchers number the protestors at twenty-four million worldwide, which makes them the largest mass protest in history, period.

In Minneapolis, the city where Floyd was killed, and where the 2020 protests began, protestors trashed a Target and destroyed plenty of other businesses. They burned police cars. Toppled other cars. Defaced buildings. People were being beaten. This kind of violence was echoed in major cities all over the country. Of course, there were many people engaged in civil disobedience, too, but the more riotous kind brought me back to my mother's anger at her sister passing, to her banging herself against the wall. As the protests went on, though, I came to realize that even some of this action was coordinated, with solutions in mind. I started seeing people who'd been protesting showing up at community meetings and giving well-informed speeches about abolishing or defunding the police to reinvest the money in schools and community programs.

And I saw that shaking things up was actually working. People started tearing down Confederate statues, which led to institutions taking down their own statues. Every company you could think of was making a statement on the importance of black lives. The longer the protests went on, the more I recognized them as the dividend-paying rebellions that they are.

The 1963 March on Washington might be most famous for Dr. Martin Luther King Jr.'s "I Have a Dream" speech, but it's also notable because the march had a specific agenda. That agenda—or list of demands, if you will—was read by activist Bayard Rustin, the deputy director of the march, from the steps of the Lincoln Memorial. I list them all below so you can read them and ask yourself, which of them, after fifty-seven years, have been met for black people:

1. Comprehensive and effective civil rights legislation from the present Congress—without compromise or filibuster—to guarantee all Americans: Access to all public accommodations, Decent housing, Adequate and integrated education, The right to vote

2. Withholding of Federal funds from all programs in which discrimination exists.

3. Desegregation of all school districts in 1963.

4. Enforcement of the Fourteenth Amendment—reducing Congressional representation of states where citizens are disfranchised.

5. A new Executive Order banning discrimination in all housing supported by federal funds.

6. Authority for the Attorney General to institute injunctive suits when any Constitutional right is violated.

7. A massive federal program to train and place all unemployed workers—Negro and white—on meaningful and dignified jobs at decent wages.

8. A national minimum wage act that will give all Americans a decent standard of living. (Government surveys show that anything less than $2.00 an hour fails to do this.)

9. A broadened Fair Labor Standards Act to include all areas of employment which are presently excluded.

10. A federal Fair Employment Practices Act barring

> discrimination by federal, state, and municipal governments, and by employers, contractors, employment agencies, and trade unions.

The March on Washington, as you can see, had a whole lot of aims. As well they should have. Black people were in a bad, bad place in 1963. But looking at all the evidence I've been laying down, name one of those demands that couldn't be applied to the current state of things, too. The agenda hasn't much changed because, well, the plight of black folks hasn't. But hey—they didn't have the power of the internet behind them then. We can do this.

LET'S GET UNCOMFORTABLE

What are the sparks that ignite protests, riots, rebellions? Where are the lines between them today? And beyond that—what's *worth it* to create real change?

This is an uncomfortable conversation because it has to do with power and perspective. As I've been saying, there's often no difference whatsoever between a riot or a rebellion besides who's looking at it and labeling it. It's also uncomfortable because it involves the question of whether the only "right" response is a totally non-violent one.

In the 1960s' civil rights movement, we had MLK and his argument for non-violent civil disobedience, and that was effective. But the 1960s famously had another civil rights leader: Malcolm X. Early in his career, Malcolm X preached "by-any-means-necessary" tactics in the fight for racial equality. The fact is, both kinds of protest helped to bring about that decade's hard-won change. I'm in no way saying violence is necessary to create progress—but while it's easy to condemn the latter, we also have to look at who is doing the condemning and the justifications for protest in the first place.

As long as systemic racism exists, you can best believe there will be the need for people to protest it. Remember what they said in the Declaration of Independence: "In every stage of these Oppressions

We have Petitioned for Redress in the most humble terms: Our repeated Petitions have been answered only by repeated injury." Protest, riots, revolts have always been responses to repeated injury. They're also how some of the most healing, humane change has happened in this country.

This chapter's title comes from the late civil rights hero John Lewis, who had this to say about the fight for equality: "Do not get lost in a sea of despair. Be hopeful, be optimistic. Our struggle is not the struggle of a day, a week, a month, or a year; it is the struggle of a lifetime. Never, ever be afraid to make some noise and get in good trouble, necessary trouble." Addressing the hurt at the root of today's protests is going to take much dialogue and much action. Let's get in trouble.

TALK IT, WALK IT

There are so many ways to fight for equality. You can march. Or you can write. You can sing, like twelve-year-old Keedron Bryant, who released an honestly killer song called "I Just Wanna Live" with proceeds to support the Black Lives Matter movement. Whatever you do, just make sure that you are sincere about staying committed.

What you can do right now is educate yourself on the history of civil unrest, not just in America but internationally. Look at what happened in South Africa to end apartheid; look at pro-democracy protests in China, at the Arab Spring movement in Egypt, and elsewhere. I encourage you to visit the Black Lives Matter home page: blacklivesmatter.com. Read *X: A Novel* by Kekla Magoon and Ilyasah Shabazz, and *The Autobiography of Malcolm X* by Malcolm X and Alex Haley. There are some great documentaries on protests or civil rights—for example, the *Eyes on the Prize* series on the civil rights movement is an excellent one.

If there's a protest in your area on a cause you feel passionate about, first, speak with your parents about it. If you can protest as a family, that's great. But sometimes that may not be possible. If you get the green light from your folks to go with friends, be smart and be safe. It's never a good idea to go to a protest alone, so make sure you practice the buddy system if your grown-ups aren't protesting with you. By *buddy system*, I mean that you should go with friends and you all plan to stay together the entire time. Sometimes protests can get chaotic. So make sure you and your buddies plan a spot to meet up at just in case one of you gets separated from the group.

Also, expect to see police officers at the protest and know how to interact with them. It's never a good idea to disrespect police officers, so don't. Make sure you obey the law and commands from law enforcement. If you're stopped by police, remain calm, polite, and respectful. Keep your hands in plain view and follow the officer's commands. Never under any circumstance should you run from a police officer.

Protesting is a powerful tool for change. For more

information on how to do it safely, check out these helpful links:

- teenhealthcare.org/blog/teen-protest-safety/
- teenvogue.com/story/how-to-prepare-protest

Unfortunately, people are sometimes arrested while protesting. If your family has the resources, talk to them about donating to one of the many bail funds, which help protestors get out of jail. You can find a national directory here: communityjusticeexchange .org/nbfn-directory. Look up the Google Doc created by Black Lives Matter activist Sarafina Nance, which directs people to meaningful places to support the movement. Find out if there are plans to build any private prisons in your state and oppose them. Find out if the police in your state are wearing body cameras (ncsl.org/research/civil-and-criminal-justice /body-worn-cameras-interactive-graphic.aspx) and/or if there are laws regarding cameras that have already been proposed.

You can also talk with your family about supporting efforts to defund the police. To clarify: Defunding the police doesn't mean abolishing the police, though there are more radical calls for that, too. It instead means redirecting money from police budgets to other government agencies funded by the city. Defunding the police could mean more money for underfunded schools, for mental health programs, or for drug recovery programs, all of which can help to reduce crime.

Before anyone says there's little chance of that happening and much less working, let me share with you that about a decade ago, Camden, New Jersey—a city once ranked number one on the FBI's list of violent crimes, with a murder rate as high as that of Honduras—disbanded its police force and then rebuilt with an entirely new one under county control, using a number of now celebrated progressive police reforms. Let me share that, after the protest in Minneapolis, their city council made a historic pledge to dismantle the local police department and shift that money to community-based strategies. Let me share that New York and LA have also committed to cutting their police budgets. (As well they should; the NYPD's budget is $5.5 billion, so big that if you were to compare it to other countries—yes, *countries*—it would make it the thirty-sixth-largest defense budget in the world. The *world*!)

We've got to think that grand. Finishing the work of protests in America is tantamount to finishing off racism. It's a big order: the biggest order. Which is why we need all the good people to fight, fight, fight injustice and inequality wherever you find it.

*"What do I do when I
think an adult is racist?"*

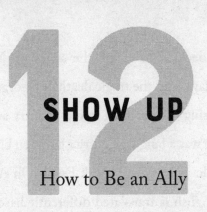

SHOW UP

12

How to Be an Ally

I want you to know that in the last days and
hours of my life you inspired me. You filled me
with hope about the next chapter of the great
American story when you used your power to
make a difference in our society. Millions of
people motivated simply by human compassion
laid down the burdens of division. Around
the country and the world you set aside race,
class, age, language and nationality to demand
respect for human dignity.

—REPRESENTATIVE JOHN LEWIS,
op-ed, The New York Times, *July 2020*

Young folks, you may already know that this book
grew out of a viral video series, and no, it wasn't a

TikTok. I decided to create the series on May 28, 2020, just days after the tragic death of George Floyd. I was assessing the problem in our country and I realized there was a language barrier between black and white people. Sure, we all speak English in America, but that English is translated differently based upon your color and culture. Many of you are studying foreign languages in class right now; I encourage you to ask your Spanish teacher how you can become fluent in Spanish. They'll probably tell you that you need to study abroad and immerse yourself in Spanish, speak with Spanish-speaking friends, or listen to Latino music, but those things alone won't make you fluent in Spanish. Because I was immersed in white culture growing up, I fully understand how to communicate with my white brothers and sisters while also being fully capable of communicating with my black brothers and sisters.

But following the murder of George Floyd, some of my white friends not so fluent in black culture had questions. Some of the questions were well-intentioned. Others, not so much. White people, I learned, didn't understand what was going on across the country or within the black community. They didn't understand the history, the hurt, or the pain that they saw bleeding into cities and towns around the country. The video series was my way of educating them and, hopefully, building up future allies in fighting off the virus of racism in America (we'll talk more about allies later).

When the idea first hit me, I imagined it would be like this: A few black friends and I would sit at a table with white people willing to ask questions about race, and we would answer those questions.

But I couldn't get a group together. Remember, this was May of 2020. The year of not only racial upheaval but a worldwide pandemic. People all over the country (really, the world) were avoiding group gatherings and travel. And my friends are scattered all over, so it would have been difficult under non-pandemic circumstances. But thankfully, I have a very close white friend who was all-in. "Manny," she'd said (that's what my white friends call me), "we need to do something. I want you to know that I am here for you. Use me however you need. Let's do something."

I explained the video idea, and she was like, "Sure, you got it.'" She drove the three hours from Dallas to Austin, Texas, and dove in immediately. We went over the questions I wanted her to ask. Questions like why are people rioting, how come black people can say the N-word but white people can't, all the good stuff—we talked through everything, we rehearsed all day. My friend's mom is a history teacher, so we hopped on an hour-long phone call with her to discuss the questions and rehearse. After a quick dinner, we rehearsed again on a FaceTime call with her sister. Her sister was a little worried that my friend might look stupid as the white woman asking these questions. The concern was noted, but we were determined to move forward the next day.

Obviously, both of us were nervous. I was nervous because this could be something big and hopefully get a lot of people listening. She was nervous because there are a lot of white people who just don't understand the black experience in America. She grew up in Dallas, which was being rocked at the time by both riots and (white) panic about the riots.

I woke up the next morning anxious but still confident, ready to have this conversation. We were due in the studio by 11:00 A.M. At 9:54 A.M., I came downstairs in my house to find her with tears in her eyes, overcome by emotion. "I just can't do this," she said. "It's just not right. You should do it without me. They don't wanna see me. They want to see you. I can't do this."

So I did it alone.

Just me, speaking into the camera to the millions of viewers I hoped would watch the video, learn, and empathize with black people's pain.

If you've read this far into the book, I hope you are

interested in being an ally. Or in the least curious about what an ally really is. Or maybe you're wondering how you can prove you're an ally in more than words? Wherever you're at, don't worry, I got you. I'll give you my sense of how necessary allies are to the fight against racism and inequality. Since the beginning of racial hierarchy in this country (remember Bacon's Rebellion from chapter 1?), this fight has always needed white people in the trenches with us, and that hasn't changed.

LET'S REWIND

Why don't we get started with a good working definition for *ally*? This one comes from Racial Equity Tools (racialequitytools.org):

> *Someone who makes the commitment and effort to recognize their privilege (based on gender, race, sexual identity, etc.) and works in solidarity with oppressed groups in the struggle for justice. Allies understand that it is in their own*

> *interest to end all forms of oppression,*
> *even those from which they may benefit*
> *in concrete ways. Allies commit to reduc-*
> *ing their own complicity or collusion in*
> *oppression of those groups and invest in*
> *strengthening their own knowledge and*
> *awareness of oppression.*

The simple version is that an ally is a person from an empowered group who acts to help an oppressed group, even if it costs them the benefits of their power.

Now that you're an aspiring (never stop aspiring) ally, a little on the legacy you're joining. In America, allyship goes back to the white abolitionist, who from the 1820s until the start of the Civil War called on the American government to ban slavery. Arguably, the most famous of these was William Lloyd Garrison, who became the head of the American Anti-Slavery Society and founded the abolitionist newspaper *The Liberator*. From the 1830s until the end of the Civil War, Garrison, at one point a close associate of Frederick Douglass, dedicated his work to the cause of ending slavery. A more radical ally was John Brown, the man who said he "knew the proud and hard hearts of the slave-holders, and that they would never consent to give up their slaves, till they felt a big stick about their heads." He staged armed rebellions like Bleeding Kansas in 1856, and the infamous raid at Harpers Ferry, Virginia, that failed when the last twenty-five or so of Brown's men were overwhelmed by marines. (I am in no way advocating that kind of violence, peoples, but we have to learn our history.)

Like I've said, after the Civil War, the South developed Black Codes and Pig Laws, which became Jim Crow laws. A lesser-known but no less dedicated ally lived in Jim Crow Alabama. Her name was Juliette Hampton Morgan. Morgan was a seventh-generation high-society Alabamian who, while riding on segregated buses in the late 1930s, began to speak out against the unfair treatment of black people and writing op-ed letters to her local newspaper. That allyship cost Morgan her job and caused her much public and private criticism. Morgan got a new job and eventually kept fighting the good fight for the civil rights of black people—this was more than fifteen years before the Montgomery, Alabama, bus boycott that helped kick off the civil rights movement. Morgan fielded threatening letters and telephone calls and had the mayor call for her to be fired from her second job. She lost friends and colleagues. Even her own mother quit talking to her; hateful people burned a cross in her front yard. She resigned from her second job in 1956, and the very next day, she committed suicide. Morgan left a note behind that said, "I am not going to cause any more trouble to anybody." Morgan endured a lot of anger and hatred in her allyship with the black freedom struggle. Imagine how much more she could have done if she'd had the support of other allies? Perhaps, even, her story would have had a happier ending.

Since I'm an athlete, Peter Norman's allyship holds a special place for me. A little over ten years after

Morgan's death, Norman represented Australia in track and field in the 1968 Olympics in Mexico City. He won the silver medal in the two-hundred-meter sprint between two Americans: Tommie Smith and John Carlos, the gold and bronze medalists, respectively. Smith and Carlos told Norman about their plan to stage a protest during the medal ceremony by raising gloved fists in a Black Power salute. When Carlos realized he forgot his glove, it was Norman who suggested they split the pair and wear one on each hand. Norman also persuaded a fellow Australian teammate to give him a small badge that read OLYMPIC PROJECT FOR HUMAN RIGHTS, an organization that had been set up to oppose racism in sports.

Smith and Carlos were immediately sent home and banned from the Olympics. But they also received a heroes' welcome from the black community once they got back to America. Norman was not so lucky when he returned home: Despite being Australia's number-one sprinter—his time of 20.06 seconds is still the

Australian two-hundred-meter sprint record—his allyship got him ejected from the world of Australian track and field and branded him a social pariah in his home country.

Another story of allyship that's close to my heart is that of Chris Long. In 2017 Malcolm Jenkins was a safety (the defensive player who plays behind the line of scrimmage and whose job it is to keep the offense from scoring at all costs) for the Philadelphia Eagles and had been very active and vocal in his leadership around Black Lives Matter. Chris Long, a white defensive end on the team, stood by Jenkins. When Malcolm raised his fist up, Long raised his fist up or put his hand on Malcolm's shoulder. It's one thing for a black person to raise their fist. They've got a lot more incentive to do so. It's a whole other statement when the white person is standing there raising their fist as well. Long standing with Jenkins was huge. Up to that point, the NFL had been largely unsupportive of Colin Kaepernick, the NFL player who began the peaceful protests in 2016, as well as Black Lives Matter protests in general.

Now that I've brought the history of allyship up to the present day, let me tell you what you don't want it to become. What you don't want your allyship to become is a white savior complex. A white savior is a white person who acts to help non-white people, but in a context that can be perceived as self-serving. A white savior is someone motivated by thinking something like this: *I have to save black people because without me, they won't be able to save themselves.*

Don't let this be you, good peoples. The white savior looks sexy in the movies, like in *Hidden Figures* when the Kevin Costner character smashes a "colored bathroom" sign—a moment that never happened in real life—or in *The Help*, with Emma Stone's character writing down the experiences of black maids and gaining credit for an act of civil rights activism. Maybe the most famous of all fictional white saviors is Atticus Finch, the lawyer who defends a black man accused of sexually assaulting a white woman in *To Kill a Mockingbird*. I know these stories were moving and may be things you really enjoyed. But trust me, there's a real danger in centering our narratives of racial struggle on well-intentioned white people, one articulated well by writer Teju Cole in his essay "The White Savior Industrial Complex." Cole writes, "What innocent heroes don't always understand is that they play a useful role for people who have much more cynical motives. The White Savior Industrial Complex is a valve for releasing the unbearable pressures that build in a system built on pillage"—a.k.a. a way for white people to say, "Look, we got you. See the good deed so-and-so white person just did to help your people? Everything is okay now, so let us stay in control. The way things are is fine again. After all, we know what's good for you better than you know yourselves." The white savior complex is a convenient way for white people to believe that white supremacy and the privilege that comes with it are not the problem when it comes to achieving racial justice but actually the solution.

You might not be able to control the powers that be, but you can make sure that your allyship comes from a pure place. Do good work, but don't make the mistake of seeking out gratitude or praise or caring more about your intentions than the *impact* of your intentions. Make sure you aren't engaged in performative allyship—the kind that goes only so far as it takes to get the right post for social media. True allyship is a commitment to fight this fight for the long haul— long after it ceases to be a top-of-the-fold news item, long after the cameras have stopped capturing it. Not today, but tomorrow, next week, next year, next decade.

LET'S GET UNCOMFORTABLE

The conversations of allyship start with the self, with those tough internal monologues. Here are some of the questions you should be asking of yourself. How are you as a white person holding other white people accountable? If you hear a white person use the N-word, call them out on it. If your classmate is being treated unfairly, speak up for them, call attention to it. Make sure you have white people in your life who will hold you accountable, too.

True allyship demands that it move from conversation to action. And that action will include risks. This isn't the 1830s, or the 1930s or 1950s, or 1968, but I won't lie to you and say it'll be easy. The risks might be something as small as a distant social media friend unfriending you. But it could be something more severe, like ostracism from an intimate friend group, job insecurity, public or private ridicule, friction with loved ones. There's the small, small chance of what happened to Heather Heyer, the ally hit by a car and killed in Charlottesville, Virginia, happening to you. Know that when you are saying you are an ally, you are saying that you are willing to risk your white privilege in the name of justice and equality for marginalized voices.

I'm from Texas—which they call the Lone Star State. But the truth is, black people can't do it by our lonesome. We need white people to take on the role of co-conspirators, confronting the issue of racism and oppression in your own circles of influence. In the story I mentioned to start the chapter, when my friend said she couldn't do it that morning, I tried to encourage her. But in the end, she had a change of heart. I don't know what happened overnight, but I guess she was tossing and turning until 4:00 A.M., woke up, and felt differently.

But that didn't mean I didn't have to pick up the slack; after our chat, I had forty minutes to figure out how I was gonna do this video by myself. When I got to the studio, I put my head down. The videographer counted me down, *three, two, one.* I lifted my head up, I stared dead into the lens of the camera, and I began my nine-minute, twenty-seven-second monologue, which, within two weeks of going live, got twenty-five million views and led to the creation of this book.

What I learned from my friend's choice was that being an ally is tricky. She had done a lot right; she reached out, drove all that way, and prepared for hours with me because of her desire to be an ally. And yet, when I needed her most, when I needed her in that moment to just sit there with me and have this conversation, she wasn't there. And though I've forgiven her, that broke my heart. Black people don't have the luxury to have a change of heart. It might not have been the world depending on me, but I didn't know who needed my voice, so I wasn't going to back down. After all, I was technically acting as an ally, too. Even though I am a black man living in America, my parents are from Nigeria. Therefore, I don't carry the same ancestral history of slavery that black Americans do. But I recognized that I could use my privilege to show up and speak up on what was happening in that moment. The lesson here is that being an ally means showing up.

LET'S KEEP IT GOING

We started this chapter with John Lewis, with the last piece he wrote before passing away. Note how he made a point to celebrate those now demanding change for "set[ting] aside race, class, age, language and nationality." You heard the man—he wants you in the game, too.

Other ways to be an ally are, really, everything I've suggested in the chapters up to now. Think about your community and the people in your life. Do most of your friends at school look like you? Change that if you can. Do you hear people in your school say racist things about people of color? Speak up. Challenge their racism with truth. Is there a protest happening close to or in your city? Show up with a few buddies; see how it feels. You don't have to lead a march (yet), but participate, maybe step outside your comfort zone, and join in the chant. Talk to your friends and family, even the stubborn ones, about race.

Finally, take care that whatever work you do is in counsel with black people. Make sure those people tell you the truth and that you commit to hearing them out all the way, no matter how uncomfortable it might make you feel. Remember, if you're reading this, I'm counting you as an aspiring ally. Starting wherever you are is okay. Heck, reading this book is a great choice. Every protest you attend, each time you stick up for a black person at school, every person with whom you have a real conversation about race, all of those things are marks in the win column. The important thing is to just keep showing up.

"*Why do we have to wait for something awful to happen to talk about racism? How do we get comfortable talking about it all the time?*"

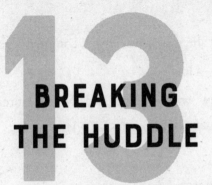

BREAKING
THE HUDDLE

How to End Racism

Young peoples, most of you probably haven't picked up a novel by the giant of American literature Toni Morrison yet. But when you do, boy, are you in for a treat! Toni Morrison (may she rest in peace) was a black woman novelist, who, starting in the 1970s, dared to write books about black people as full human beings at a time when most "serious" literature was written by and about white people (not much has changed today, unfortunately). Morrison's books often dealt with family, love, race, and racism. And whenever she was interviewed, comments about race came up—a lot.

Interview with author and Nobel laureate Toni Morrison, *The Colbert Report*, 2014:

STEPHEN COLBERT: *I don't see race.*

TONI MORRISON: *[chuckles]*

COLBERT: *I've evolved beyond racism. I don't see race. I don't even see my own. People tell me I'm white, and I believe them because I haven't read any of your books. [audience laughter] But can I, as a white man, understand the African American experience?*

MORRISON: *Well, you have to know something about racism.*

COLBERT: *But then wouldn't I be a racist if I thought about racism?*

MORRISON: *Perhaps. But more important than that, is [that] there is no such thing as race.*

COLBERT: *Really?*

MORRISON: *It's just a human race. Scientifically, anthropologically. Racism is a construct—a social construct. And it has benefits; money can be made off it. People who don't like themselves can feel better because of it. It can describe certain kinds of behavior that are wrong or misleading. So, it has a social function. Racism.*

But no race. Race can only be defined as a human being.

September 21, 2014. Picture me in my first game starting as middle linebacker for the Philadelphia Eagles. We're playing against the Washington Redskins—who in 2020, after public pressure, dropped the belittling term *redskin* from their name—at home, and there's a midnight-green sea of tens of thousands in the stands of Lincoln Financial Field. I trot out onto the bermuda grass, listening to the defensive coach bark the play through the headset in my helmet. I take a knee, feeling my heart pumping with nerves (it's only the third game of my second season), feeling the heat of my teammates as they wait for me to relay what to do.

You see, as a middle linebacker, it's my job to gather the other ten players into the huddle and call the play. Every single player has a responsibility, although what's called in the huddle means different things to different players based on their positions. It's without doubt an important part of the game. But see, here's the thing. Nobody comes to a game to see the players huddle. They come to see the players execute the plays that are called in the huddle. The way I see it, this book is like the huddle. I've announced the plays, and while the chapters may speak to different readers in different ways, the time is almost here for all of us to go run the play. Because ultimately, it's not about the huddle; it's about what you do after you break.

We're about to break, my friends.

But one more story first. During the coronavirus pandemic, I've tried to find ways to work out outside of a gym, and one of them has been biking. The problem is I haven't biked since I was like twelve, and I'm now thirty. Still, I went to the store one day and got myself a nice bike. My first time out, I was super excited to ride, extremely excited. I took it into the scorching Austin heat. I'd bought a little bike helmet to go with my new ride. I had my bike gloves. You couldn't tell me I wasn't a Tour de France winner.

I rode around my neighborhood, and everything was fine, just fine, till I tried to bike up a steep hill. I couldn't get up. I pedaled hard, but I just couldn't make it. So I got off and started walking. And then I took another lap and tried to ride back up. Once again, I couldn't make it up. I was determined not to let the hill beat me, Mr. Former Middle Linebacker. And then I saw one of my neighbors, and they were like, "Hey, you might have an easier time if you shift the gears." *Um . . . why didn't I think of that?* Well, I hadn't thought of it because, despite my fancy bike and all my equipment, I hadn't ridden a bike in a long time. I'd forgotten there was a gear shifter on the bike. Soon as I lowered the gear, I was finally able to pedal up the hill.

Is it even possible to end racism? I bet you've been wondering, and you're not alone. It's not an easy answer, but I think it involves looking for the gears we haven't used yet.

Long ago, plenty of people believed that slavery would never end. Before 2008, plenty of people believed it was impossible for a man named Barack Hussein Obama to be president of the United States.

The irony is that some of those same people hailed President Obama as the symbol of post-racial America once he assumed office. I never bought it; heralding a post-racial America was also like saying the work of ending racism was done, like we could take off our pads, hit the locker room showers, and go celebrate the victory. But that work has never been done. Racism has been shape-shifting for decades, and fighting it demands vigilance against its many changing forms.

Still. Though it's been with us for almost four hundred years and is as adaptable as anything I can think of—the fact that it was man-made gives me faith that we can still yet undo it. Not in our lifetime, maybe not in anyone's lifetime. It's important not to let that discourage you, but rather encourage you to stay in this long, noble fight.

LET'S REWIND

All right, before we break this huddle, let's run it from the top. The racism I've covered in this book falls into three basic categories. The first is individual—the acts and expressions of discrimination, stereotyping, ignorance, or hate one person can level at another—and is broadly what we covered in part 1. The second level is systemic racism: the unfair policies, practices, and procedures of institutions that produce racially inequitable outcomes for black people and POC, while also yielding advantages for white people. You remember part 2. The third level of racism is a little different; it doesn't map onto part 3; rather, it runs through and under a lot of the pain in this book. That's internalized racism: when people of color support white privilege and power, or when they're driven to doubt who they are, or doubt each other, or accept the status quo. This is everything from me as a kid wondering if I was "black enough," to black actors fighting over the few roles open to them in Hollywood in order to be "the one," to black people who use positions of power to support racist policies or attitudes. It is every bit as linked to the effects of white racism as everything else we've covered, and is part of what needs to change.

I started this book talking about how important language is to black identity and how you should always strive to find the right language to identify a black person (*black* is my preferred, if ever we should meet). We covered white privilege, that invisible but ever-present advantage for white people, how it works like the benefit of the doubt, how it makes whiteness the default normal. We added cultural appropriation, which in America is, in essence, white people plagiarizing the culture of an oppressed group. Not okay—but also an opportunity to look for ways of engaging with and learning about other cultures without stealing or stereotyping. Speaking of stereotypes, we spent some time with the Angry Black Man. Now, speaking to my young white brothers and sisters: Ladies, please, please, don't grow up to be a Karen. Don't threaten to call the police on a black person for little to no reason. And gents, don't grow into men literally weaponizing your whiteness. Don't! And none of y'all better be using the N-word. Also, make sure you don't tell your black friends, "You don't talk like you're black" or "You don't dress like you're black" just because they sound intelligent or dress in a certain way.

When it comes to systemic racism, remember that in America it goes back four centuries to when the first Africans arrived on these shores and links up through the advantages still enjoyed by white people in almost every area of society—education, housing, and employment, to name a few. Recall that there's no such thing as reverse racism. Yeah, a black person can be racist individually (see chapter 8), but black people as a whole don't have enough power in America to effect systemic racism. Black people have had that power seized from them in a Fix secured by tactics including voter suppression and jury-rigging. Our biased criminal justice system works hand in hand with the stereotype of black men as inherently dangerous, as thugs and gang members—which leads to over-policing, over-incarceration, and yet more bias in the justice system.

Black people being murdered by law enforcement, specifically, is what led to the formation of Black Lives Matter in 2013, a crusade to end police brutality and achieve social equality for black people. In many ways, it follows in the footsteps of other movements in this country aimed at obtaining true freedom for black people—the abolitionist movement and the civil rights movement being two of them. In all of those campaigns, black people have needed white allies, white people who've been willing to take on the issue of oppression and racism as their own, even when it means giving up some of their privileges.

When the first Africans arrived in 1619 in Virginia, there was no such thing as a white person. As far as the law is concerned, white people as a race didn't exist until 1681, when colonial American lawmakers sought to outlaw marriages between European people and others. Before that, people were known by their nation of origin, what we might now refer to as *nationality* or *ethnicity*. Anti-miscegenation laws, the laws prohibiting Europeans from marrying (and having children with) people of African descent, forged the white race. Let's think about what this means. Race was a political creation, an economic creation— all this hate developed to secure the interest of some seventeenth-century dudes who wanted to get rich growing sugarcane and cotton, who wanted to make sure they'd always be the class on top. Which is to say, racism has always been about power. Which is to say, we invented racism. Which is to say, maybe we can learn to uninvent it, too.

Let me tell you what the movement for racial equality can't afford: white allies being fragile about racial issues. The premise of this book is about putting those issues on the table, about engaging with tough conversations, about my white brothers and sisters having to sit with the discomfort because that's how progress is made. This is not to say I want to intentionally hurt a white person's feelings. On the contrary, I want to move us toward healing. But we can't get to that part without the hard truths being a part of it.

If you are raising white kids, please, please talk to them about race. We must all see color to see racism. Plus, color, ethnicity is part of what makes people human, and to deny any of us our particularity is to deny our humanity. And as Toni Morrison said, race is, if nothing else, human.

LET'S GET UNCOMFORTABLE

The heart of this book has been a conversation. Hopefully, as you've been reading, you've been having those tough conversations with the people that are close to you, about race, about class, about politics. Hopefully, too, you've been talking to black people. Hopefully, you are listening to them, even when it makes you a little squeamish. And if you find that you can't come to some agreement, I hope that you disagree respectfully.

White privilege can assert itself in conversation in a few ways, so stay wary. As a white person, never dominate the discussion, and try not to respond by reframing or reinterpreting what a black person or POC is saying. Instead of telling someone to "calm down" if they are passionately recounting a racially charged incident, take a pause yourself and try to empathize with their feelings and work hard to hear them. And try not to change the topic of race-based discussions to other forms of privilege. For example, if a black friend is talking about a racist comment made by another student, don't pivot the conversation in that moment to talk about your experiences with bullying. This is not to say that other forms of oppression aren't valid, and indeed we need to have all of those conversations. It's just to say that the focus should be on the subject at hand until your friend has had a chance to speak their part. And also, this is not a competition to see who is more oppressed.

TALK IT, WALK IT

I want to close with telling you about my best friend, Brittany. She's a white girl, in her twenties, blond hair, born and raised in Austin, Texas. She's so different from me. Whenever I do something that just makes her shake her head, she always says, "Oh, *bless*," in a Southern country accent. And it's usually something about which I'd simply say, "You trippin'." The truth is Brittany and I live life together as extremely close friends not only despite but in celebration of our differences—because I look at her whiteness, and I appreciate the beauty that comes with the person. And she looks at me and my blackness and my culture, and she appreciates the beauty that comes with that. We don't try to change the other person. We just smile and laugh with, and sometimes at, the other person.

As I think about what a country or world without racism might look like, I'm reminded of June 14,

2020. Little did I know that Brittany and one of my other closest friends, a black girl named Mo, had conspired to throw me a surprise party. It was a party to celebrate me moving to Los Angeles for a new job. I was sitting at the house of one of my old friends, Andy, just reminiscing on my time in Austin, when Brit and Mo called to tell me some weird odor was coming from my house. I desperately had to get back home, they said, like fifteen minutes across town. I was like, "Guys, whatever it is, I'm not worried." But they insisted, "You got to handle this immediately."

Andy and I hugged and shed a couple of tears, and I sped home to investigate a mystery smell, which in hindsight really made no sense. I walked into my house and saw Brittany. And she was like, "Hurry up, come around the corner. Here it is." And as I turned the corner, I heard, "Surprise!"

There were maybe sixteen or seventeen smiling faces looking at me, all of my dearest friends in Austin wishing me goodbye. Of that friend group, of about seventeen people, eight of them were white. Some of them were pastors, small-group leaders, strength coaches in Austin. And of that group of about seventeen people, seven of them were black. There were a couple of former and current professional athletes. One person was mixed race, and another was Mexican. And they were all gathered in my house with smiles on their faces as we celebrated. Mind you, this was in the midst of shooting episode 3 of *Uncomfortable Conversations with a Black Man*. I realized that I was living out what I'm promoting on the show. Because in that room were white people and black people and Mexican people and mixed people, and we were all there eating and laughing and talking and enjoying each other's good company.

We were all also wearing masks since it was still during the coronavirus (2020, am I right?). But at one point, we took off our masks for a second to take a picture together. My aim is that life looks a lot like the group of seventeen people gathered around my kitchen island with smiles on their faces, living life together at my surprise party. A world without racism is being in one country, on one continent, in one world celebrating life together, wherever we've come from to get there.

Ending racism is not a finish line that we will cross. It's a road we'll travel.

ACKNOWLEDGMENTS

I think this is the part of the book where I'm supposed to say thank you to all of the instrumental people who helped me create *Uncomfortable Conversations with a Black Man* and the children's edition, *Uncomfortable Conversations with a Black Boy*. It's almost like an acceptance speech. Which, by the way, I've never been good at giving because I didn't really win a lot growing up, but here goes nothing!

To you, yes you, the reader. Thank YOU. This book, this project, the sleepless nights, arthritic fingers, and bruised vocal cords are well worth it because you have chosen to take a first step toward making our world a better place. So thank you for sitting at this table with me, for having this conversation, and for motivating me to keep going, even when I was tempted to stop.

Oprah, I can honestly say I never thought I would be thanking you in my life, particularly because I never thought we would speak or that you would know who I am. However, I have quickly realized that good people are attracted to good things. Thank you for stopping what you were doing just to hop on the phone with me in the middle of a pandemic and hear my heart. I've played team sports my whole life, and I can confidently say that you're one of the best team-mates I've ever had.

Mitch, the man who put his life on pause, dropping everything to help me make my dream come true. I'm glad you checked your Twitter direct messages that day, because if not, the world may not have this book now. You're an incredible thinker, an incredible writer, and an unsung hero. Thank you, my friend.

Meghan, when we first met on Zoom and they told me, "She's going to be your best friend over the next few months," I was like, "Yeah, right." Well, yeah, they were right. You responded to questions at all hours; challenged my thoughts for the better; and in-terjected your pure and genuine, well, whiteness. You made one of the scariest tasks, writing a book, pretty manageable.

Mekisha, for your help sharing my vision with the next generation. For making sure we didn't sugar-coat anything and trusting our readers will be brave enough to listen. For getting my book in the library of every school in the country. Well, consider that a challenge!

Meredith, it took you some convincing at first (don't worry, y'all; I'll tell that story in another book), but after you realized that the world could be inspired by my voice on this topic, you moved full speed ahead and made yourself readily available. Thanks for tolerating me and my madness, and thank you for helping to make this book come alive.

Terry, you saw in me what I hadn't yet seen in myself: the passion and ability to bring a positive message to the world. Thanks for believing in me.

Rachel, thanks for talking through this idea with me. After the murder of George Floyd, I wasn't sure what I was going to do, but I knew I needed to do something. When I asked you to join me, you were more than willing. When COVID-19 had other plans, you encouraged me and my ability to move forward even without you.

Taylor, you were right: "Uncomfortable Conversations" does sound a lot better than "Questions White People Have." This conversation went much further than we ever could've imagined while sitting at my kitchen table. Everything happens for a reason.

Mo, I'm forever grateful for you. You've been there through every episode of the show, and every page of the book. Before this was ever a book, when it was simply an outline and I had stayed up for twenty-four hours (falling asleep on the keyboard), you picked up where I left off and helped me make sentences out of gibberish. When I was too nervous to eat, because I knew the potential weight these words could carry, you made sure I was taking care of myself while I attempted to help so many. Maybe this book could have been written without you, but I don't want to imagine how. Thank you.

To my brother Sam, you inspire me, encourage me, and motivate me. Everything I do, I try to do excellently because of you. You're my biggest inspiration, and I love you more than you know. Thanks for setting the bar so high; you've made me a better man and a better human.

Steph, your love for me doesn't go unnoticed. You've always wanted to see me win, and you were the first one to speak my current reality of life into existence. Thanks for believing in me before there was much to believe in.

Chichi, you're forever one of my favorite humans on the earth. When my life got chaotic, our conversations about nothing and everything all at the same time kept me sane. I can't imagine my life without you. You're the best.

Dad, I got my ability to communicate from you. The reason my words have resonated with so many is because of what I caught and was taught by you growing up. Thank you for the sacrifices you made for me, putting me in a position to try to change the world. You taught me how to work and how to sacrifice. You taught me how to deliver truth with grace and love. I am who I am because of you.

Mom, you're an angel walking the earth. If Dad taught me how to communicate, you taught me how to have compassion. Thanks for being my biggest cheerleader and biggest supporter. Thanks for always making sure that your youngest son felt loved and taken care of. I love you.

Lastly, I end this book the way I start every episode of *Uncomfortable Conversations with a Black Man* and anything I do of significance: by thanking God. I've consistently referred to this season in my life as my "Esther moment" (Esther 4:14). I'm honored that God equipped and called me to be a messenger in this moment. Jesus's love for me has set the bar for the way in which I'm called to love people, and the way in which I'm called to love you, the reader.

I'm humbled to have been able to write this book and facilitate this message, and I'm grateful that you chose to come on this journey with me.

Let's continue to change the world, together. I love y'all.

QUICK TALKS

In the NFL, you have a playbook, and your play-book has every play you could ever need on defense. Probably close to ninety to a hundred different plays. Different formations. Different variations. Different adjustments. During my time on the Eagles, my coach, Rick Minter, would hand out what was called the *LB (Linebacker) Tip Sheet*. It was about twelve pages thick, stapled, your name and your number on the front, and inside a reminder of all the plays we'd learned from that week. At the very back of the tip sheet, the last two pages or so, was "things to look out for." These were things that may not have been what we had practiced all week but that we might see in the game the next day.

That's what this little bonus chapter is. There are all sorts of "things to look out for" in the road to anti-racist allyship, and also, I'm gonna be real—a lot of things I've gotten questions about that I didn't get to cover in other chapters. We may not have talked about the below topics at length, but I'm giving you this little tip sheet because you might see them in the game of life.

LEXICON

Before I give up the goods, let me say that everything I'm talking about is a part of black culture. And while black culture is different from white culture, me providing you with explanations is not about saying black culture is somehow weird, exotic, in need of explaining. Black culture is not below white culture, and this isn't a safari. But black culture is, in many respects, different from white culture. And while you're reading this, keep in mind that white people have had the benefit of having their culture become the mainstream. Black people have never been the mainstream, and whatever chances they've had for their culture to become popular, they haven't been anywhere near as long-standing or come as often as they have for white people.

TERMS

It seems like a simple and obvious point, but I'll say it anyhow: In order for you to know what black culture is, you'll have to know the definition of *culture*. Google the word *culture* and you'll find a whole heap of definitions out there, but for the sake of keeping it simple, I'll use anthropologist Bronisław Malinowski's definition. Malinowski describes culture as a "well organized unity divided into two fundamental aspects—a body of artifacts and a system of customs." To clarify, cultures are things made by a group of people and also a way of doing things.

The second word that I want you to have a handle on is *diaspora*. A *diaspora* is a dispersion of a people, language, or culture that was formerly concentrated in one place, to scatter, to displace, to live in separated communities. So in the case of black people, the African diaspora includes black people and their descendants who are living off the continent. All black people in America are part of the African diaspora. There's a white diaspora, too, though Europeans don't use the term as much. One important thing to remember is that Africans were mostly forced into their dispersion, while in America, the Europeans mostly came of their own volition (and also, of course, sans chains). Another important thing to remember is the diaspora holds a multitude of cultures. Okay, I hope that was clear and helpful. Now to the tip sheet.

BLACK NAMES

One day when I was working for ESPN, a colleague and I were on a break from shooting, and he asked me, "Hey, bro, I really would love if you just answer for me, like why do black people have the most unique names? Like white people, we have names like Steven and Dan or Sarah or Britney or Anna, but black people, you have Carmelos; you have LaMichaels; you have LeBrons. You have so many unique names." Well, black names are definitely a thing. But the first thing I'll say is that they aren't weird. They just aren't accepted as the mainstream.

To understand black names, we must be aware that, during slavery, black people took on the surnames of their enslavers. We must note as well that, while black people lost almost all their autonomy during slavery, many of them retained the ability to name their kids, that naming kids was an important means of establishing a black person's place in their community, was a means of keeping track of family members who were sometimes (often) sent elsewhere. After emancipation, black people kept up the practice of choosing special names. However, the people who did it were always a small few, like under 5 percent. Long before there was Latasha or LeBron or Jaden or Shaniqua, there were Booker and Perlie. In fact, in the 1920 census, 99 percent of all the men with the first name of Booker were black, as were 89 percent of all men named Perlie. Names like Tyrone, Darnell, and Kareem were popping during the civil rights movement.

According to an ABC News poll, among the top black names for girls currently are Imani, Ebony, and Precious. Among the top black names for boys are DeShawn, DeAndre, and Marquis. Another fun fact about the evolution of names: Historically, the more black people use them, the less white people use them.

BLACK WOMEN'S HAIR

Look, I'm the first to admit that I don't know everything about black women's hair, but I do know a thing or two. One thing I know is that for some black women, their hair is a crown. Another thing I know is that you'd better not touch a black woman's hair without permission. If you go to New York's famous 125th Street in Harlem, and walk east to west, you're liable to see some black women, usually African women, sitting outside of a salon, calling out to women who are passing by, "Miss, miss. You want to get your hair braided?" There's a reason that these are black women who do this, a reason that you'll likely never see a white hair stylist doing the same thing. Because black women's untouchable hair is a huge part of black culture.

It goes back far. Check the Ancient Egyptian hieroglyphs and you'll see images of dreadlocks, Afros, and box braids, styles we still use today. While twisted locs have roots in ancient Hindu culture, they are a huge part of African culture. In some parts of Nigeria—shout-out to my peoples—braids can communicate things like age, religion, whether a person is married or not, and where they stand in a tribe hierarchy. And there are styles upon styles upon styles. The Bantu knots, which are big with the Zulus of South Africa. Braids are also an African cultural tradition that managed to endure while black people were enslaved. Like cornrows, which not only represented black folks' homeland but also helped protect people's hair while they were out toiling in the fields. Braids still serve some of the same purposes today. Plenty of black women wear them to protect their hair, even braiding synthetic hair to give it greater protection or for style. If you remember only one thing from what I said, remember that many black women love their hair and that it's theirs alone.

DURAGS

If this were another part of the book, I'd tell you about how, up until the slave trade, many African men wore their hair long—it was a sign of many positive things, life experience, social position within a tribe, and so on, among them. I would tell you that when Africans got to America, white people who were intent on erasing their culture, keeping their hair clean, and maximizing output started making them wear their hair short. I'd tell you about how black men have gone through all kinds of popular hair styles since emancipation, from the conk, to the Afro, to the Jheri curl, to the fade. If this were an earlier part of the book, I'd get into all of that history . . . but since it isn't, I'll get to the part I really want to talk about, which is waves. My waves.

Waves are the kink of black people's hair smoothed out with grease and brushing. And man, when I was a kid, especially when I was in middle school and high school, having waves in my head was like having the latest throwback jersey or some brand-new Jordans; it was like how it is now for a grown man to own a Rolex. To get waves, I had to wear a wave cap, had to slick my hair down at all hours, really all hours when I wasn't around white people. Well, the thing that I called a *wave cap* was also called a *durag*. No one truly knows who invented the durag, but a guy named Darren Dowdy, president of So Many Waves, claims that his father, William J. Dowdy, invented it in the late 1970s as part of a wave kit. Inventor credit aside, it's been an essential part of many a young person's quest for waves, as it helps compress them. But it evolved out of its practical means to become a hip-hop fashion staple. Dudes have worn them untied under a baseball cap. Or with the strings tied to the back. Or with the strings tied to the front. Durag as fashion was never my thing, for the record, but when you see them, know that there's a lot going on there.

SAGGING

When I was in high school, I used to have to wear a uniform. And a part of my uniform was making sure my pants were pulled up on my waist and belted. At the same time, I used to watch people like Allen Iverson in the NBA, who not only wore his clothes super big but wore his pants low on his waist. That was the style back then, but my private school wasn't going for that, and neither were my parents. Now that I'm grown, I still don't sag—just not my thing. But there's no denying that sagging is a part of black culture.

What I didn't know way back when was that sagging came out of prison (maybe the adults did, and that's why they were so adamant against it). In prison, because they can be used as weapons or in suicides, belts are off-limits. Since prison uniforms aren't all that concerned with fit either, incarcerated humans have been known to walk around with pants too big in the waist—hence the sagging. Sooner or later, most guys get released. And those guys reentering the free world still didn't wear belts. That's how the fad of sagging caught on outside of the prisons. Before long, young people were doing it, and their parents were admonishing them, which is a perfect recipe for them doing it even more. A word for the unwise who are thinking about taking on this particular aspect of black culture: Sagging has been linked to hip and lower-back problems. If that isn't enough discouragement, I offer you some words from the coolest president who ever lived. "Brothers should pull up their pants," said Barack Obama in a 2008 MTV interview. "You are walking by your mother, your grandmother, your underwear is showing. What's wrong with that? Come on. Some people might not want to see your underwear. I'm one of them." Personally, to my black brothers—you do you. And white peoples, don't be telling us different—not your place. But yeah, I'm not gonna be showing my grandma my boxers.

LOTION

"What's the deal with black people and lotion?" one of my white friends asked. I could've responded with the science again, told him that our skin acts as a barrier to the outside world and that it works best when it's moisturized. I could have told them that the deal with black folks and lotion is that black folks seem to have heeded this science more seriously. I didn't get into all that; what I told him was that dry skin shows up more prominently on people with darker skin, shows up as a whitish coloring that we call *ash* (picture the ash after a volcano). What I told him was that you don't want to be caught ashy if you're black. If we call another black person *ashy*, it means we can see the dry skin, and it's a huge faux pas.

To fight the ash, black people use copious amounts of lotion, often carry lotions with them. I saw this video on Twitter the other day of a father getting his really young son ready for school. The father took a big gob of Vaseline and spread it all over the boy's face. When he was done, the boy looked slick as licked Popsicles. Vaseline is popular; so is cocoa butter or shea butter or, in some rare cases, actual butter. What white people also need to understand, or not, about lotioning is that it is a cultural practice that is passed down from generation to generation. And this knowledge includes learning the spots on one's body with a high probability for ash: ankles, elbows, knees, and hands. Missing one of those spots leaves us open to teasing and/or to implying that we aren't taking care of ourselves. Neither of which is a good conclusion. So yeah, lotion, is high on our list of self-care priorities. You won't get me out here ashy.

BLACK DON'T CRACK

One of my white woman friends came up to me one day and asked me about the phrase "Black don't crack." She thought it was just a figure of speech. Well, it is and it isn't. "Black don't crack" is like an anthropology and science quiz all in one. Per the anthropology part, when those early humans left the continent of Africa, some of them migrated to colder regions and adapted with less melanin (and other adaptations suited for colder regions). So goes the science, the darker your skin, the larger the pockets in the skin cells. Those pockets are called *melanosomes* and contain melanin. If you're pasty, you have very little melanin. If you're Asian, you produce a yellow kind of melanin called *phaeomelanin*.

Black people produced the darkest, thickest melanin of any group. It's called *eumelanin*. Melanin absorbs and scatters more of the sun's rays, which means the more of it you have, the more protection you have from those rays. Any dermatologist worth their salt can tell you there are two factors that cause skin aging—natural aging and photoaging. I hate to break it to you, but unless you got a time machine, there's nothing you can do about natural aging, but photoaging, which is caused by the sun, well, that's another thing. The more protection your skin or some aid gives you from the sun, the better you will age. Hence the phrase "Black don't crack" for us dark peoples.

RECOMMENDATIONS

BOOKS

Anderson, Carol, and Tonya Bolden. *We Are Not Yet Equal: Understanding Our Racial Divide*. New York: Bloomsbury, 2018.

Bieschke, Marke. *Into the Streets: A Young Person's Visual History of Protest in the United States*. Minneapolis, MN: Zest Books, 2020.

Cherry-Paul, Sonja, Jason Reynolds, and Ibram X. Kendi. *STAMPED (for Kids): Racism, Antiracism, and You*. New York: Little, Brown, 2021.

Gates, Henry Louis, Jr., and Tonya Bolden. *Dark Sky Rising: Reconstruction and the Dawn of Jim Crow*. New York: Scholastic Focus, 2019.

Jewell, Tiffany. *This Book Is Anti-Racist: 20 Lessons on How to Wake Up, Take Action, and Do the Work*. Minneapolis, MN: Frances Lincoln Children's Books, 2020.

Reynolds, Jason, and Ibram X. Kendi. *STAMPED: Racism, Antiracism, and You*. New York: Little, Brown, 2020.

Stevenson, Bryan A. *Just Mercy (Adapted for Young Adults): A True Story of the Fight for Justice*. New York: Delacorte Press, 2018.

Stone, Nic. *Dear Justyce*. New York: Crown Books for Young Readers, 2020.

Zoboi, Ibi, and Yusef Salaam. *Punching the Air*. Waterville, ME: Thorndike Press, 2020.

WEBSITES

"Find Your Polling Place: Voting Information Tool." Vote.org: vote.org
/polling-place-locator.

"How, Where, and When to Vote: Absentee and Early Voting." USA.
gov: usa.gov/absentee-voting.

Mallett, Kandist. "What to Know Before Heading to a Protest." Black
Canary, *Teen Vogue*, May 29, 2020. teenvogue.com/story/how-to
-prepare-protest.

McCarey, Daniel. "Teen Protest Safety: How Young People Should
Prepare to Protest." Mount Sinai Adolescent Health Center, June 19,
2020. teenhealthcare.org/blog/teen-protest-safety.

Racial Equity Tools: racialequitytools.org.

We Need Diverse Books: diversebooks.org.

DOCUMENTARIES AND MOVIES ABOUT BLACK HISTORY, RACE, AND RACISM

YOUTUBE

"How America Invented Race." *The History of White People in
America*. World Channel, premiered July 6, 2020. youtube.com
/watch?v=ppvbBY3ce8Y.

"Official Trailer: *The History of White People in America*." World
Channel, premiered June 30, 2020. youtube.com/playlist?list=PL
-7a7eUvdMmiijPA1MauPmMpAEtN50_Go.

PUBLIC BROADCASTING SERVICE

Eyes on the Prize: America's Civil Rights Movement. American Experience, aired October 2, 2006. pbs.org/wgbh/americanexperience/films/eyesontheprize.

KPBS. *The African Americans: Many Rivers to Cross.* 2013. video.kpbs.org/show/african-americans-many-rivers-cross.

KPBS. *The Talk: Race in America.* Aired February 20, 2017. video.kpbs.org/video/talk-race-america-talk-race-america.

NETFLIX

When They See Us.

REFERENCES

1: ROLL CALL

Taylor, Derrick Bryson. "George Floyd Protests: A Timeline." *The New York Times*, January 6, 2021. nytimes.com/article/george-floyd -protests-timeline.html.

2: WHAT DO YOU SEE WHEN YOU SEE ME?

ABC News. "Referee's Questionable Call for Wrestler to Cut Dreadlocks." *ABC News*, n.d. abcnews.go.com/GMA/News/video/referees- questionable-call-wrestler-cut-dreadlocks-59971992.

Washington, Jesse. "The Untold Story of Wrestler Andrew Johnson's Dreadlocks." *The Undefeated*, September 18, 2019. theundefeated.com/ features/the-untold-story-of-wrestler-andrew-johnsons-dreadlocks.

3: THE HEAD START

Scruggs, Afi-Odelia E. "Colorblindness: The New Racism." *Teaching Tolerance*, Issue 36, Fall 2009. tolerance.org/magazine/fall-2009 /colorblindness-the-new-racism.

4: CITE YOUR SOURCES OR DROP THE CLASS

Clifton, Derrick. "Five Reasons Katy Perry Is Pop Music's Worst Cultural Appropriator." *Mic*, August 1, 2014. mic.com/articles/95444/5 -reasons-katy-perry-is-pop-music-s-worst-cultural-appropriator.

Fears, Danika. "Katy Perry's Geisha-Inspired AMAs Performance Stirs Controversy." *Today*, November 25, 2013. today.com/style /katy-perrys-geisha-inspired-amas-performance-stirs-controversy -2D11650791.

Wilson, Julee. "Katy Perry Apologizes for Cultural Appropriation, Rocking Cornrows." *Essence*, June 14, 2017. essence.com/hair/katy -perry-apologizes-cultural-appropriation.

5: THE MYTHICAL ME

Ebert, Roger. "*The Birth of a Nation*." *RogerEbert.com*, posted March 30, 2003. rogerebert.com/reviews/great-movie-the-birth-of-a -nation-1915.

"Indoctrinate." *Learner's Dictionary*, Merriam-Webster, n.d. learnersdictionary.com/definition/indoctrinate.

Keyes, Allison. "A Long-Lost Manuscript Contains a Searing Eyewitness Account of the Tulsa Race Massacre of 1921." *Smithsonian*, May 27, 2016. smithsonianmag.com/smithsonian-institution/long -lost-manuscript-contains-searing-eyewitness-account-tulsa-race -massacre-1921-180959251.

Pérez-Peña, Richard. "Woman Linked to 1955 Emmett Till Murder Tells Historian Her Claims Were False." *The New York Times*, January 27, 2017. nytimes.com/2017/01/27/us/emmett-till-lynching-carolyn -bryant-donham.html.

"*The Birth of a Nation* (1915)." IMDB.com, n.d. imdb.com/title /tt0004972.

6: NOOOOOPE!

Elitou, Tweety. "Trevor Noah's Suggestion That Rappers Remove the N-Word from Their Lyrics Has the Entire Internet Arguing." *BET*, October 26, 2019. bet.com/celebrities/news/2019/10/26/trevor -noah-suggests-rappers-remove-the-n-word-from-their-lyrics.html.

Shaw, A. R. "Trevor Noah Says Rap Music Does Not Give White

People Right to Use N-Word." *PostNewsGroup*, October 25, 2019.
postnewsgroup.com/trevor-noah-says-rap-music-does-not-give
-white-people-right-to-use-n-word.

7: THE GAME IS RIGGED

"Black Codes and Pig Laws." *Slavery by Another Name*, n.d. pbs.org/tpt
/slavery-by-another-name/themes/black-codes.

Brown, Anna, and Atske, Sara. "Blacks Have Made Gains in U.S.
Political Leadership, but Gaps Remain." Pew Research Center,
January 18, 2019. pewresearch.org/fact-tank/2019/01/18/blacks
-have-made-gains-in-u-s-political-leadership-but-gaps-remain.

Coski, John. "Myths and Misunderstandings: The Confederate Flag."
American Civil War Museum, January 9, 2018. acwm.org/blog
/myths-misunderstandings-confederate-flag.

Franklin, Alexandra, Ryan Deal, and Breland Coleman. "What Is
Convict Leasing?" *Sugar Land Convict Leasing*, 2018. exhibits.library
.rice.edu/exhibits/show/sugarlandconvictleasing/history-of-convict
-leasing.

Gerdeman, Dina. "Minorities Who 'Whiten' Job Resumes Get More
Interviews." *Working Knowledge*, Harvard Business School, May 17,
2017. hbswk.hbs.edu/item/minorities-who-whiten-job-resumes
-get-more-interviews.

Hager, Eli. "A Mass Incarceration Mystery." The Marshall Project,
December 15, 2017. themarshallproject.org/2017/12/15/a-mass
-incarceration-mystery.

"Key Events in Black Higher Education." *The Journal of Blacks in Higher
Education*, n.d. jbhe.com/chronology.

Losen, Daniel J., and Paul Martinez. "Executive Summary." *Lost Opportunities: How Disparate School Discipline Continues to Drive Differences in the Opportunity to Learn*, October 2020. Palo Alto, CA/ Los Angeles: Learning Policy Institute; Center for Civil Rights Remedies at the Civil Rights Project, UCLA. civilrightsproject.ucla .edu/research/k-12-education/school-discipline/lost-opportunities -how-disparate-school-discipline-continues-to-drive-differences-in -the-opportunity-to-learn/Lost-Opportunities_v12_EXECUTIVE -SUMMARY.pdf.

"Study Finds White Teachers of Black Students More Likely to Punish Students for Misbehavior." *The Journal of Blacks in Higher Education*, February 4, 2019. jbhe.com/2019/02/study-finds-white-teachers-of -black-students-more-likely-to-punish-students-for-misbehavior.

8: STANDING UP TO YOUR BULLIES

Dahlen, Sarah Park. "Picture This: Diversity in Children's Books 2018 Infographic." *Musings on Korean Diaspora, Children's Literature, and Adoption*, June 19, 2019. readingspark.wordpress.com/2019/06/19 /picture-this-diversity-in-childrens-books-2018-infographic/.

"Equity vs. Equality: What's the Difference?" Milken Institute School of Public Health, George Washington University, November 5, 2020 .onlinepublichealth.gwu.edu/resources/equity-vs-equality.

Lopez, German. "Why You Should Stop Saying 'All Lives Matter,' Explained in Nine Different Ways." *Vox*, July 11, 2016. vox .com/2016/7/11/12136140/black-all-lives-matter.

9: THE FIX

Glass, Andrew. "Bush Declared Electoral Victor Over Gore, Dec. 12, 2000." *Politico*, December 12, 2018. politico.com/story/2018/12/12 /scotus-declares-bush-electoral-victor-dec-12-2000-1054202.

Keyssar, Alexander. *The Right to Vote: The Contested History of Democracy in the United States*. New York: Basic Books, 2000.

Krieg, Gregory. "It's Official: Clinton Swamps Trump in Popular Vote." CNN, December 22, 2016. cnn.com/2016/12/21/politics/donald -trump-hillary-clinton-popular-vote-final-count/index.html.

"Rebuilding the South After the War." *Reconstruction: The Second Civil War*. American Experience, aired January 12, 2004. pbs.org/wgbh /americanexperience/features/reconstruction-rebuilding-south -after-war.

10: THUG LIFE

Abbey, Jennifer, Candace Smith, and Matt Rosenbaum. "Chicago Gang Life: Gang Members Talks [*sic*] About Life on the Streets, Heartache." *ABC News*, October 17, 2012. abcnews .go.com/US/chicago-gang-life-gang-members-talks-life-streets /story?id=17499354.

11: GOOD TROUBLE

Desmond-Harris, Jenée. "Are Black Communities Overpoliced or Underpoliced? Both." *Vox*, April 14, 2015. vox .com/2015/4/14/8411733/black-community-policing-crime.

"Nash, Diane Judith: Biography: May 15, 1938." *Martin Luther King, Jr. Encyclopedia*, n.d. kinginstitute.stanford.edu/encyclopedia/nash -diane-judith.

"Sit-Ins: Event: February 1, 1960." *Martin Luther King, Jr. Encyclopedia*, n.d. kinginstitute.stanford.edu/encyclopedia/sit-ins.

Zucchino, David. "The 1898 Wilmington Massacre Is an Essential Lesson in How State Violence Has Targeted Black Americans."

Time, July 1, 2020. time.com/5861644/1898-wilmington-massacre
-essential-lesson-state-violence.

12: SHOW UP

"Juliette Hampton Morgan: A White Woman Who Understood."
Teaching Tolerance, n.d. tolerance.org/classroom-resources/tolerance
-lessons/juliette-hampton-morgan-a-white-woman-who-understood.

Pelissero, Tom. "Chris Long: Attention I've Received Shows Power
of Protests." NFL.com, August 22, 2017. nfl.com/news
/chris-long-attention-i-ve-received-shows-power-of-protests
-0ap3000000833295.

13: BREAKING THE HUDDLE

Aptheker, Herbert. "The History of Anti-Racism in the United States."
Black Scholar 6, no. 5 (1975): 16–22. doi.org/10.1080/00064246
.1975.11413695.

Busette, Camille. "Mayors and Governors: This Is How You Tackle
Racism." *How We Rise* (blog). Brookings, June 2, 2020. www
.brookings.edu/blog/how-we-rise/2020/06/02/mayor-and-governors
-this-is-how-you-tackle-racism/.

"Can We Talk? Tips for Respectful Conversations in Schools, Workplaces
and Communities." Anti-Defamation League. Accessed August 1,
2020. www.adl.org/education/resources/tools-and-strategies/can-we
-talk-tips-for-respectful-conversations-in-schools.

Edgoose, Jennifer, Andrea Anderson, Joedrecka Brown Speights, Katura
Bullock, Warren Ferguson, Kathryn Fraser, et al. "Toolkit for
Teaching About Racism in the Context of Persistent Health and
Healthcare Disparities." Society of Teachers of Family Medicine

Resource Library, September 18, 2018. resourcelibrary.stfm.org
/viewdocument/toolkit-for-teaching-about-racism-i.

"Key Terms ~ Race and Racism." Vanderbilt University. Accessed
August 1, 2020. www. vanderbilt.edu/oacs/wp-content/uploads/sites
/140/Key-Terms-Racism.pdf.

McCammon, Sarah. "Want to Have Better Conversations About Racism
with Your Parents? Here's How." NPR, June 15, 2020. www.npr.org
/2020/06/09/873054935/want-to-have-better-conversations-about
-racism-with-your-parents-heres-how.

McIntosh, Kriston, Emily Moss, Ryan Nunn, and Jay Shambaugh.
"Examining the Black-White Wealth Gap." *Up Front* (blog).
Brookings, February 27, 2020. www.brookings.edu/blog/up-front
/2020/02/27/examining-the-black-white-wealth-gap/.

McWhorter, John. "The Dehumanizing Condescension of *White
Fragility*." *Atlantic*, July 15, 2020. www.theatlantic.com/ideas/archive
/2020/07/dehumanizing-condescension-white-fragility/614146/.

"Racial Justice, Racial Equity, and Anti-Racism Reading List." Harvard
Kennedy School. Accessed August 1, 2020. www.hks.harvard.edu
/faculty-research/library-knowledge-services/collections/diversity
-inclusion-belonging/anti-racist.

"Toni Morrison." *The Colbert Report*. Comedy Central, November 19,
2014. www.cc.com/video/9yc4ry/the-colbert-report-toni-morrison.

Wijeyesinghe, C. L., P. Griffin, and B. Love. "Racism Curriculum
Design." In *Teaching for Diversity and Social Justice: A Sourcebook*,
edited by M. Adams, L. A. Bell, and P. Griffin, 82–109. New York:
Routledge, 1997.

ABOUT THE AUTHOR

Emmanuel Acho grew up in Dallas, Texas with his three siblings and his Nigerian immigrant parents. In 2012, he was drafted into the NFL to play for the Cleveland Browns and later the Philadelphia Eagles. He has a master's degree in sport psychology from the University of Texas. In 2016, he left the NFL for ESPN, where he served as the youngest national football analyst, and was named in the 2018 Forbes 30 Under 30 list. He is now a Fox Sports Analyst and the creator of the online video series *Uncomfortable Conversations with a Black Man.*